SEE YOURSELF IN A NEW LIGHT

PRACTICAL TIPS, EXERCISES, AND POSITIVE AFFIRMATIONS FOR WOMEN TO RECOVER SELF-WORTH, CULTIVATE SELF-LOVE AND BOOST SELF-CONFIDENCE

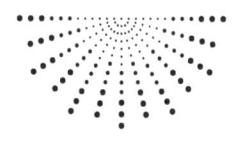

SARRANA RAIN

Registration Number TX 9 - 139 -400

© Copyright 2022 ARVIE IGUANA LTD —All rights reserved.

Legal Notice:

This book is copyright protected. It is not legal to reproduce, duplicate, or transmit any part of this document in either electronic means or printed format. Recording of this publication is strictly prohibited and any storage of this document is not allowed unless with written permission from the publisher.

This book is only for personal use. You cannot amend, distribute, sell, use, quote or paraphrase any part, or the content within this book, without the consent of the author or publisher except for the use of brief quotations in a book review.

Disclaimer Notice:

Please note the information contained within this document is for educational and entertainment purposes only. All effort has been executed to present accurate, up to date, and reliable, complete information. No warranties of any kind are declared or implied. Readers acknowledge that the author is not engaged in rendering legal, financial, medical or professional advice. The content within this book has been derived from various sources. Please consult a licensed professional before attempting any techniques outlined in this book.

Under no circumstances will any blame or legal responsibility be held against the publisher, or author, for any damages, reparation, or monetary loss due to the information contained within this book. Either directly or indirectly. You are responsible for your own choices, actions, and results.

CONTENTS

See Yourself In A New Light	vii
A Special Gift To Our Readers	ix
The Author	xi
Introduction: Making a Change	xiii

1. WHY WE NEED SELF-ESTEEM (AND HOW TO BEGIN MANIFESTING IT) — 1
   What if it Doesn't "Click"? — 10

2. SEE YOURSELF AND RECOGNIZE YOUR WORTH — 13
   Affirmations and Self Esteem — 14
   Inner Peace and Acceptance — 17
   Know Your Strength — 19
   Exercise — 20

3. BELIEVE IN YOURSELF (BY KNOWING WHERE YOUR SELF ESTEEM IS LOCATED AND HOW TO FEED IT) — 21
   Self-Belief Affirmations — 34
   Affirmations to Boost Your Confidence — 35
   Affirmations to Raise Your Inner Voice — 35
   Affirmations for Charisma — 36
   Exercise — 37

4. LEVEL UP YOUR CONFIDENCE — 39
   Take Risks and Build Endurance — 47
   Have Fun with Power Poses! — 48
   Be Goal-Oriented — 49
   More Formulas For Growing Your Self-Confidence and Self-Esteem — 49
   Growth Mindset — 53
   Women and Confidence in the Workplace — 54

Affirmations	56
Exercise	59

5. RAISE YOUR INNER VOICE — 61
Assertiveness: Why You Deserve to Occupy Space	64
Shyness and Social Phobia	70
What Causes Shyness and Social Phobias?	71
What Perpetuates These Patterns?	74
Recognizing Patterns of Unhelpful Thinking	77
Ways to Challenge an Unhelpful Thought	79
Additional Activity: Use and Abuse the Points System!	81
Affirmations	82
Exercise	84

6. FACE YOUR FEARS — 85
Why DO We Fear?	86
Fear of Rejection	90
Responding to Criticism	93
Fear of Failure	96
How To Cope With Fear of Failure	97
Handling Your Mistakes (and How to Move On)	99
Affirmations	101
Exercise	102

7. SELF-COMPASSION AND SELF-LOVE — 103
What are Self-Love and Self-Compassion?	103
Why We Put Ourselves Last	105
Self-Love Deficit Disorder	108
What is Self-Love Abundance, and How Can You Work Towards It?	110
50 Ways to Put Yourself First (and Practice Self-Love and Self-Compassion)	112
Affirmations	116
Exercise	118

8. LOVE YOUR BODY — 119
Why Some Women Feel Bad About Their Appearance (and Why They Shouldn't!) — 120
Historical and Cultural Perceptions of Beauty (and Their Influence) — 122
Body Image, Self Esteem, and Mental Health — 124
Social Media and Self-Image — 126
My Journey — 127
Affirmations — 130
Exercise — 132

Final Words — 133

9. MEDITATION SCRIPTS TO KEEP FOR LIFE — 135

☀ *It's Time to Take My Destiny into My Own Hands…* — 139
☀ *I Understand the Importance of Self-Confidence, Self-Love, and Self-Esteem* — 141
☀ *I Am Prepared to See Myself for Who I Truly Am* — 143
☀ *I Believe in My Capabilities* — 145
☀ *I Have a Voice, and I Am Going to Use it Loudly, Proudly, and Without Apology* — 147
☀ *There Are Things in this World that Frighten Me…* — 149
☀ *Self-Compassion Can Be Difficult* — 151
☀ *I Love My Body Exactly as It Is* — 153
☀ *I Am Enough; I Am Good Enough* — 155

We Need Your Help! — 159
Acknowledgments — 163
Another Book You Need — 165
References — 167

SEE YOURSELF IN A NEW LIGHT

PRACTICAL TIPS, EXERCISES, AND POSITIVE AFFIRMATIONS FOR WOMEN TO RECOVER SELF-WORTH, CULTIVATE SELF-LOVE AND BOOST SELF-CONFIDENCE

Plus 9 Bonus Self-Esteem Meditation Scripts to Keep for a Lifetime, So You Never Have to Worry You're Not Good Enough

Sarrana Rain

A SPECIAL GIFT TO OUR READERS

Included with your purchase of this book is a copy of our listicle, *How To Be You.*

If you somehow feel discontented with what you have or discouraged because you believe you are unworthy, not enough, not capable, think again.

If you think you need to keep up, be 'some' one to be accepted, to be valuable, to be loved, think again.

Discover THE SECRET to achieving pure happiness and unfaltering confidence given the pressure of our new generation's evolving social scripts and standards through this mini-book, How To Be You.

It is a good read for you and for all the women you care about.

Stop living someone else's life.

Live not FOR someone but for YOU, for your happiness and your cause.

Scan the QR code or visit the link below and let us know which email address to deliver it to.

http://sarrana-rain.com/ |

https://arvieiguanaltd.activehosted.com/f/3

VISION

*Changing how women see themselves, their circumstances,
their surroundings, the people,
the shifts, turmoils, and devastations inside and outside their circles, as
well as their view of the grand scheme of things in a new light,
is what it takes to open up a better world for them.
A world where they are allowed to take up space,
where their fluid mind is free to create and innovate,
and their liberated spirit is empowered to initiate actions to create an
even better world.*

*A world of compassion wherein they can strive to hone their abilities and
uniqueness, live mindfully with inner peace,
make things happen with courage and will,
be themselves the master of their own self—
gentle but dauntless, resilient and driven, exist with a sense of purpose,
cultivate love for self and others,
respect self while respecting others.*

THE AUTHOR

Sarrana Rain is an umbrella name representing not one but a number of brilliant and exceptional writers who share the same vision and mission as the founder: to empower women. They are authors who want to make a difference alight with a fierce desire to help every woman, anywhere, uplift herself.

Sarrana Rain will never allow you to sink into the mire. She will polish you until you shine with your innate and glorious light.

INTRODUCTION: MAKING A CHANGE

I remember the day I knew I needed to change.

The bar was stuffy and crowded. I sat alone on my stool and watched all the confident, happy people having more fun than me. Their body heat condensed and dripped down my glass. I'd been stood up again. I know now that a woman's worth should never hinge on a man's approval. Yet, at the time, I had little confidence. The rejection stung—deeply. I wiped my sweaty palms on my dress, paid, and waited in tears for my taxi. I felt lonely. Unintelligent. Unattractive. Unwanted. It was the straw that broke the camel's back.

And the saddest thing about it?

My place in the world was completely wrong.

There had to be a reason—me, right?

Fortunately, I've moved past it. If you've ever felt this way, you're not alone. Sometimes the world can be unkind to women. Patriarchy taught us that, to be feminine, we must be beautiful, educated, and maternal in a specific way.

Our shoulder devil whispers that we are too ugly, loud, ambitious, lazy, what have you. We're too focused on our careers or our families. We must sacrifice one for the other.

It is exhausting to please the wider world—so many conflicting messages and demands. And when we do so, we're left with no time or energy to *try to please ourselves*. How can we love ourselves in this climate? How can we silence these nagging voices? If you've been struggling with these questions, I want to reassure you—I've been where you are now.

I'd like to invite you to imagine another way.

Imagine a life in which your confidence and tranquillity come from within. Imagine waking up and designing your appearance, schedule, and lifelong goals yourself. Would you—the real, authentic you—prefer to wear bright make-up or rock it au natural? Do you enjoy having smooth skin, or do you consider shaving a chore and a waste of your time? Do you wear pastel dresses and heels? Or do you go for a rock or grunge style? What music would you listen to if you weren't afraid of what others would say about it? What jobs would you apply for? What hobbies would you enjoy? What would your perfect relationship or family look like?

What if you knew your worth at any given event? What if you enjoyed rather than feared new challenges and people? What if you could step outside of your comfort zone, knowing that it will be there for you when you return? After all, our comfort zones are only for visiting—they're not for living inside.

Imagine reaching your full potential. What if I told you there was a way to empower yourself? To lift this burden from your shoulders and experience life without fear?

It sounds too good to be true. But I'm delighted to tell you that you already hold the answer in your hands. The meditation prompts in this book, affirmations, and practical tips will unravel your best self. There's also a series of unique exercises for you to complete. This combination of emotional and practical work will be sure to work in tandem to increase your self-confidence and self-esteem.

You will cultivate genuine self-love and practice compassion for others. You will also conquer your fears and adopt a more liberated perspective.

Reverse automatic, negative thinking to improve your emotional regulation. Just to be clear, do *not* stifle your grief or pain. Ride your feelings without judgment, and don't let them master you. Then you will live a carefree life.

This book speaks to the soul.

I bless you, and I welcome you as you take this first step towards self-actualisation.

Take my hand in yours.

And let's begin.

1
WHY WE NEED SELF-ESTEEM (AND HOW TO BEGIN MANIFESTING IT)

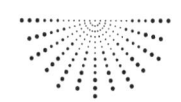

"You're not going out dressed like that, are you? It's way too revealing."
"He won't like you if you don't show a little skin."
"You're coming on a little strong, aren't you? I like modest women."
"You need to make the first move, or he won't respect you!"
"Women should always be pretty and well-groomed."
"You're not a real feminist if you shave your legs or wear make-up."
"Hi, sweetheart. Can I talk to a professional, please? Like, a man?"
"Hello, ma'am. Is your husband home? I need to talk to the head of the house."
"But how are you supposed to focus on a career if you have children?"
"But how are you supposed to focus on raising children if you have a career?"
"Oh this is not a place for a woman"
"She came off too aggressive."
"She came off too meek."

"She's too fat."
"She's too skinny."
"Her skin is too dark." "... not fair enough" "... too pale."
"... too much tattoo."
" She's too short."
" She's too tall."
"He left because she isn't good enough."
"He left because she's too good, too much."

And so it goes on—ad nauseam.

Hands up if you've ever heard these messages or a variation of them? That's pretty much most, if not all of us, right? Many women suffer from poor self-image and self-esteem. We're assaulted with these conflicting patriarchal messages day after day. They appear in our culture, media, workplaces, and even our homes. They affect us on both a conscious and a subconscious level, chipping away at our self-worth. Women everywhere are bombarded with the message that we're too much, not enough, too quiet, too loud. This has damaging long-term effects on our relationship with ourselves and the world.

We stop dressing for ourselves and seek others' approval through our skirts' lengths, shoe heights, or voice pitches. We don't advocate for ourselves in the workplace because we doubt our intelligence. Then we get passed over for raises and promotions, hence the "glass ceiling." We abandon our ambitions because they are "unimportant." Society tells us that we'd best help realize somebody *else's* dream. Low self-esteem can lead to eating disorders and dangerous bodily modifications. According to the ads, "beauty" means skinny and pale. This narrow definition excludes most women.

Worse, low self-esteem can lead women into abusive relationships. They think their abuser's manipulative and toxic "love" is all they deserve. Even when they want to leave, they don't have the strength.

The sad thing is, that abusers, rely on this to easily work at breaking their victims down.

That's why I don't blame any woman for her low spirits.

Self-esteem—called self-worth, self-regard, or self-respect by some—is essential for overcoming the challenges life throws our way. We need to protect it.

Most of the damage to our self-esteem is self-inflicted. We often respond to rejections and failures by becoming self-critical, listing all our mistakes and flaws, calling ourselves ridiculous adjectives, and beating ourselves when we're already down. We then use unrealistic justifications to degrade our self-esteem when it is already hurting, like, "It's a way to keep my expectations low," "It will keep me humble," or "It's true; I deserve it. I hate myself!"

Enough is enough.

This book is one small but powerful flagship in the revolution of female empowerment. These potent and effective de-programming techniques will undo the damage. Through positive affirmations, you can slowly reconfigure yourself.

The power of positive self-affirmation is immense.

What is a positive affirmation? This is a particular phrase that challenges ingrained, damaging patterns of ways of thinking, and then replaces them with a more mindful way of processing our world. It isn't magic: it's simple, cognitive science. Our minds are malleable. Even the right mindset can undo years of toxic messaging. Find a mantra that serves you well and repeat it daily.

The effectiveness of positive self-affirmation has been proven repeatedly in psychological fields. According to research, "Self-affirmation theory argues that maintaining self-identity is not about being exceptional, perfect, or excellent" (Cohen & Sherman, 2014).

Rather, we need to be "competent and adequate in different areas that we value to be moral, flexible, and good" (Steele, 1988).

We discover our *inherent* strengths and remember them daily. Are you an excellent creative writer? A skilled accountant? A compassionate parent? A good listener to your friends? Are you an activist for a cause close to your heart? Identify your worth, and celebrate it! When you have low self-esteem, it can be difficult to believe you have *any* positive traits. But everybody does. Dig deep. Ask your friends, family, partner, or trusted co-worker what they value about you. You might be pleasantly surprised!

To be clear, self-identity shouldn't refer to one defining term or trait that describes who we are because this can be limiting—even self-destructive. If you put all your identity eggs into one basket, so to speak, you run the risk of losing your sense of self when the single trait that defines you is challenged or changed. One's identity is not rigid but fluid, and there are many aspects of your *self* that combine to make you, you.

If used consistently, studies find that positive affirmations can help individuals maintain a positive self-view and that threats to perceived self-competence can be met with resistance. When our identity feels threatened, self-affirmations can restore self-competence by allowing individuals to reflect on sources of self-worth, such as their core values (Cascio, et al., 2015).

That being said, affirmations can only work best when focused on affirming your existing values. According to Catherine Moore, you should "use your real strengths, or strengths that you consider important, to guide your affirmations" (2021).

If you're wondering how you can achieve this, don't worry. Below are seven easy steps to strengthen your sense of identity and self-worth:

1. Understand Why It's Important to Change Your Habits and Your Thoughts

To begin this journey, you have to believe in its aims and its power. Belief takes discipline. You could even physically write your motivations down if you wanted to. Why do you want to change? What has led to you having low self-esteem? What would it feel like to have happier, more loving, and more peaceful thoughts? To live without anxiety or fear? What kind of role model do you want to be to the young women around you? Who do they see—a self-assured or pressured woman? Once you understand why you want to change, you'll find it far easier to do so.

2. Don't Be Afraid to Ask for Help—From the Right People

Humans are social creatures. We evolved to seek the approval and assistance of those around us: it's written into our DNA. There is nothing wrong with relying on your loved ones. Those relationships are beautiful and nourishing. And the less alone we feel, the higher our confidence can fly. Proceed with caution. Not everybody has your best interests at heart. Some people with low self-esteem tear others down to make themselves feel better. Be fearless in eliminating toxicity and harmful messaging from your life. Don't rely on anyone who insults you. Your relationships make up a garden. Water the flowers and tear out weeds.

3. Use Affirmations and Mantras

Read this book's affirmations, but come up with your own, too! They will enhance you, no matter how silly they sound. Let them change the way you see yourself without feeling like you're twisting the truth.

4. Be Grateful for the Miracle that You Are

You are perfect, just as you are. You already have everything you need inside of you to flourish, succeed, and thrive. All this book is going to do is bring that inner self out so that the rest of the world can bask in it. Take a moment, every day, to experience gratitude for the miracle that you are. Your relationship with yourself lasts your entire life. So make it a good one. You deserve it.

5. Be Present and Mindful

When you are present and mindful, you stop sweating the small things so much. This leads to better mental and physical health. Being present means not judging yourself. No state is permanent. That goes for pain too. This betters your emotional processing.

6. Give Back and Be Humble

Give back and be humble. It's an excellent way to avoid myopia and arrogance. There is nothing more empowering than helping others. Whether it's giving to charity, volunteering, or advocating, you stay grounded.

7. Have Faith in a Higher Power

Your higher power helps you maintain perspective about life's challenges. Take succour in whatever higher power appeals to you.

Now let's have a look at how you can use your positive self-affirmations.

Step One: Connect Pen to Paper...

... and in doing so, strengthen the assertive nature of your affirmations. Keep a journal, diary, calendar, or even a string of post-it notes on your bathroom mirror. Doing so helps you better understand how you are working through the world around you. It also embeds positive messaging into your mind.

Step Two: Say It Loud, Say It Proud!

This might feel a little strange at first. It will gradually feel more natural—as it should. Set a time each day and repeat your affirmations out loud in front of a mirror.

Step Three: Harness The Power of Visualization

By using your imagination, you attract your desired outcome. Breaking your undesirable habits and replacing them with more positive ones. This creates a self-fulfilling prophecy of success. Ask for what you desire, put in the work, and the universe will be more than happy to oblige. This isn't magic. It's psychology and asserting your place in the world.

thoughts become things

WHAT IF IT DOESN'T "CLICK"?

A study titled "Positive Self-Statements: Power for Some, Peril for Others" concluded that Positive self-statements seem to provide a boost only to people with high self-esteem—those who ordinarily feel good about themselves already. The study also found that positive mantras about yourself like "I'm lovable" can backfire. For people who don't actually believe them, these personal mantras can lead them to feel worse because the affirmation reminds them of why they feel they aren't lovable (Wood, et al., 2009).

That's why we created this book, *13 Steps to Optimum Self-Esteem For Women*—so you won't miss out on this opportunity and can truly benefit from the power of positive affirmations. In *13 Steps*, we will help you work on the foundation first.

13 STEPS TO OPTIMUM SELF-ESTEEM for Women

SARRANA RAIN
A COMPLETE GUIDE TO INCREASING SELF-WORTH AND NEVER HAVING TO DOUBT YOURSELF AGAIN

LOOK INSIDE THE BOOK BY SCANNING THE CODE

> *You are a living magnet*

Positive thinking and self-belief are extremely powerful tools, and they're related to another concept that helps us bring our dreams into reality: manifestation and the Law of Attraction.

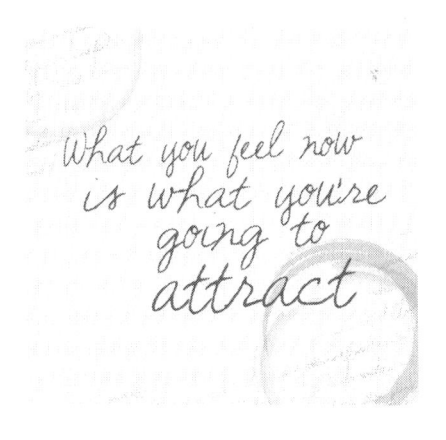

> *What you feel now is what you're going to attract*

You may have heard of the Law of Attraction—it's popular among celebrities, and Oprah, Lady Gaga, and J. Lo have all credited the practice of manifestation as a key to their success. The Law of Attraction is a simple philosophy: positive thoughts bring positive results into your life, while negative thoughts bring negative results (Scott, 2020). Manifestation works by way of *energy*, and proponents of the Law of Attraction believe that the positive energy you put out into the world manifests as a return on your investment in all areas of your life, including your health, finances, and relationships (ibid.).

Positive attracts positive

Manifestation involves consciously and deliberately applying one's thoughts toward the desired outcome. The key is to visualize yourself as you want to be: vibrant, prosperous, and surrounded by love. Speak your words of affirmation aloud and write them down in your journal—or on a post-it note, which you can see every day.

Next, take tangible steps towards achieving those desires. Would passing a test help you? Or would revamping your wardrobe do the trick? Don't worry—we'll provide more concrete examples later on.

In the next chapter, we'll take an even deeper dive into valuing yourself. And as we proceed, I want you to remember that you're doing amazing!

2
SEE YOURSELF AND RECOGNIZE YOUR WORTH

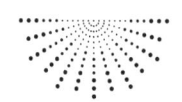

Seeing yourself for who you are is the first step toward recognizing your self-worth. Once you illuminate your soul, you can better navigate the world. Insults hurt because they shock. With self-esteem, you will meet these blows head-on and continue with your day unshaken.

LOOK AT YOURSELF

Here you'll find affirmations for self-esteem, inner peace, and bodily acceptance. Draw on them whenever you feel you need a little boost of love and positivity in any of these areas. Combine, pick and choose your favourites to incorporate them into your daily routine. You can also use them as jumping-off points for your own. Embed these powerful mantras to your entire being. Speak them aloud to enjoy their positivity and power.

AFFIRMATIONS AND SELF ESTEEM

We'll begin with some affirmations for self-esteem. If you're still having a little trouble getting to grips with the concept, that's okay! Every person's definition of self-esteem is different. Self-esteem is simply the overall subjective sense of personal worth or value.

In an article for *verywellmind*, Kendra Cherry, MS, explains that self-esteem may be defined as how much you appreciate and like yourself regardless of the circumstances and is defined by your security, self-assessment, identity, and belonging.

Your self-esteem isn't a fixed state. It can fluctuate, ebb, and flow depending on your circumstances. For example, you might have more faith in your professional life than your familial one. Thus, your sense of self is happier and more stable at work. Of course, the inverse (as well as a million other scenarios!) can be true. This is to say that a bad day, or a bad place, is simply that: in other words, it is temporary and will end. No pain or insecurity owns you or lasts forever.

What's beyond our control alters our self-esteem. What you *can* control is your reaction. The following affirmations will help with just that.

Feel free to recite each affirmation out loud yourself or silently on your head, however you feel comfortable doing so.

SELF ESTEEM AFFIRMATIONS

- I am so much more than I can see, so much more than I think I am, and so much more than I have heard about myself.
- What others think of me does not define me.
- I love noticing and acknowledging my worthiness.
- I like to see myself as a whole and unique individual.
- There is nobody exactly like me, and that is a beautiful thing.
- I see the beauty in everything, and I appreciate the small details of the world around me.
- Every day, I vow to take time to notice the things I like about myself.
- I like embracing the whole of who I am right now.
- No state is permanent—I am always growing into a truer, fuller version of myself.
- I love and respect myself deeply.
- I love knowing that I have the power to change my thought patterns.

- I love knowing that I am in control of my thought process. I control it, it does not control me.
- I love knowing that my beliefs manifest my reality.
- I vow to take the necessary action steps to manifest my dreams.
- I can achieve my goals because I am passionate, committed, and intelligent.
- Liking and respecting myself is not only easy, but it's also necessary.
- I see and appreciate my value.
- I am truly a beautiful soul; I am a wonderful human being.
- I know I am worthy.
- I know I am enough.
- I will always love and respect myself.
- Having respect for myself helps others to like and respect me.
- Today, I choose to be the most beautiful version of myself, both inside and out.

INNER PEACE AND ACCEPTANCE

Inner peace and acceptance are very powerful tools. They meet adversity with equanimity, tranquillity, and dignity. Some people undervalue or struggle with the ability to accept the world as it is. This is not the same as being defeatist. Do not let people take advantage of you or disregard difficult situations. Master your responses to imperfect situations and *harness those emotions for the better.*

If you're angry about injustice, volunteer for a local group advocating for the injured party. Draw on your strength and passion to make a positive change. This is accepting reality without letting it master you.

Below, you'll find some more examples of how peace and acceptance can sound:

- I have a natural awareness of all the positive things in my life.
- I am at peace with my mind, body, and soul.
- I am comfortable being myself.
- I see my overall strength and weakness and accept them.
- I stand tall in my uniqueness.
- If people dislike my authentic self, I can't help that, and that's okay.
- I accept that what's right for me might be met with disapproval. I am strong enough to withstand this.

- I insist that I am right because I know my action and my decision is for a good cause not only for me but for all possible living involved.
- I provide for myself, I take care of myself, and I take up space without guilt because I know that by doing so, I am not violating the rights of others.
- My heart is calm.
- The world can be a difficult and frightening place. I have the strength, power, and will to endure and overcome challenges.
- I can make positive changes to myself and others, no matter what the current reality might look like.
- I can hope and work for better life without feeling entitled to it.
- Even if at times I feel lonely, I will always have my relationship with myself to nurture and fall back on.
- There are people who love me and wish to see me thrive, even if I don't always feel that's the case. They are cheering me on when my voice is quiet.
- If a job, relationship, or goal doesn't work out, it wasn't meant to be: this is not a reflection of me or my worth.
- Nobody is watching me, hoping I make mistakes. Nobody is judging me. And if they are, the fault is with them, not with me.
- I do not exist only to make others comfortable.
- My worth is not defined by titles, money, or status. Rich or poor, single or attached, I am who I am, and that is enough. I can never be less.

KNOW YOUR STRENGTH

- Acknowledging my strengths gives me the confidence to overcome my weaknesses.
- Every day, I emphasize my positive qualities and fully appreciate my assets.
- I make the most of my unique strengths and abilities. Every day I grow stronger in mind, body, and spirit.
- I have faith in myself and my abilities.
- I have the talent I need to realize my dreams and live a fulfilled life.
- I love discovering talents and abilities that I didn't know I possessed.
- I give myself space to grow and learn.
- I know that my abilities are limitless. I have a limitless pool of talents inside me. I have the skills and gift to find success.
- I invest time and effort to increase my skills and strengthen my talents. I use my talent at work and home, so everyone benefits. I balance my pride in my gift with humility to avoid arrogance.
- I am a woman of power!

- I am strong and capable.
- Today, I follow my authentic heart and discover my true excellence.

EXERCISE

Write down ten positive things you *truly* believe about yourself, with specific examples. Dig deep! If you find this a challenge, you can ask people close to you for traits they admire and appreciate in you, but try your hardest to come up with these yourself!

For example:

I am a good girlfriend because today, I listened to my partner's worries and concerns and helped them feel validated.

I am a good writer because this week, I edited and improved my short story.

3
BELIEVE IN YOURSELF (BY KNOWING WHERE YOUR SELF ESTEEM IS LOCATED AND HOW TO FEED IT)

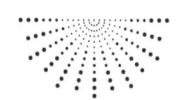

Today, the email I'd been waiting for arrived.

And it wasn't the response I wanted.

I had been rejected for a professional opportunity I'd been really excited about. I had the passion, the drive, and the relevant experience. I had tailored my application details to the very best of my ability and then had them reviewed by people close to me, just so I could rest assured in the knowledge that my application had been looked over by eyes other than my own. I made it a point to highlight why I believed I was the perfect person for this position, and I was writing my statement—committing my history, my dreams, and even some of my fears and doubts to paper, in that personal essay—I felt my heart begin to sing. Writing down these examples of what I know are my strengths, and outlining anecdotes from my past, helped me, momentarily, to see myself, or as an employer, might see me. I saw a competent, accomplished, driven woman: a woman who was articulate, burning with a desire for the greater good, and who could present herself charmingly and professionally. I was myself with my best foot forward. It was like having a mirror held up, and I liked the woman I saw looking back at me.

And then, when the rejection landed in my inbox, I came crashing back down to earth.

Suddenly, all of these positive—and true!—traits and accomplishments of mine seemed... diminished. Somehow, they were no longer in the forefront of my mind. All I could think was that I had been deemed 'unworthy.'

And, of course, because human minds are naturally inquisitive, my next thought was: why?

What was it about me that had convinced the hiring body I didn't meet the mark? Never mind the fact that the job market in any industry is always saturated—overwhelmed, even—by extremely skilled and competitive candidates. No, I wasn't in a logical enough place, at that moment, to remember that somebody else's success didn't mean my failure. In my current state of mind, I was overly focused on discovering some definitive, negative trait about myself to explain the new, gaping wound of this rejection.

And the funny thing, looking back, is that very few wounds of ours are ever 'new.' Often, we're treading familiar psychological, emotional, and spiritual paths we've been down a dozen, a hundred, a million times before: there's even a literal, neurological basis for this. Our brains use the same synapses and stress responses they've used to 'save' us from pain and rejection in the past... by flooding us with the same emotional intensity we experienced in that original moment.

If this sounds complicated or abstract, allow me to clarify. Let's say that you had an uncaring mother who, in your youth, always made a habit of putting you down. She would insult your appearance, intelligence, acumen, social skills and more daily. These millions of rejections mounted until you grew to expect nothing but rejection. More than that, you believed the horrible messaging with which you were bombarded. Now, as an adult, if you're not careful and mindful of your thought patterns and emotional responses, you might find yourself bringing that childhood hurt into romantic rejections, and perceived failures in games or sports...

Or, in my case, professional setbacks.

See, this email, to me, was a reminder that I needed to brush up on my 'cognitive training.' Our emotions and our processing skills are a little like muscles—we need to condition and maintain them to serve us in the way we want them to, which doesn't always mean letting them take the easy way. It's easy for our minds to fall back into youthful, harmful, or unproductive patterns, just as we're more comfortable when our muscles are at rest, but that doesn't mean that we're building strength. Conditioning, cardio, and discipline do that. Your brain is similar.

In this chapter, we're going to look at something called neuroplasticity. This essentially refers to how malleable and adaptable your brain is. The brain is an incredible organ—it learns and reacts at great speed, but it can also drive us to unproductive behaviours and thought patterns because it has evolved to learn that behaviours that serve us well once will be useful in a situation it recognizes as similar some time down the line. However, this can mean it doesn't always serve us in a way that is helpful in the present.

For example, if your brain perceives something as a threat, it will respond in the same way as it did when you encountered threats in the past. Let's say that you were once mugged and felt a course of adrenaline, fear, and cortisol (the stress chemical) rushing through you. Many people in this situation might freeze, feeling their hearts pound and their palms become sweaty. When you encounter something in the future that isn't as stressful as this event—say, a curt email from your boss—your brain, perceiving the threat to be of equal value, might make you emotionally and physically feel as if you are back in the situation in which you were mugged. Can you see how this is not always ideal for our everyday functioning as we move through the world around us? The same is also true of positive emotions, by the way. Our brain finds paths and narratives that it recognizes from our past and dictates our physiological and psychological responses from there.

What exactly comprises our self-esteem?

Well, there are a variety of factors that can affect it—and chip away at it. This can include, but isn't limited to, the feedback and treatment we receive from our parents (or guardians), our extended families, our teachers, peers, and other influential figures in our early life. As we grow from childhood into (hopefully) more independent adults, our spheres of influence grow and change (we go from the small, care-taking unit to the wider world of school and work); however, the common factor here is that we are always surrounded by (and conditioned to seek the approval of) other people.

This isn't a fault. Sometimes, we can feel as if we shouldn't care what others think about us, and while this is true on a basic or surface level, there is more nuance to our relationship with the social world. After all, early humans depended on group dynamics for their very survival—the desire for validation from others is hardwired into our biology. You are not 'weak' or swaying to social influence; if the positive or negative comments of those around you affect your mood—that just means you're human! A skill that you can learn, however, is to handle those feelings of joy or rejection in mindful, helpful ways —and this is very achievable!

But before we continue, is there another element—besides what we'll call, for simplicity's sake, 'nurture?'

Yes!

The physiology of your brain can have an impact on your self-esteem.

Our mood, self-perception, and emotional responses to external stimuli (like a snide comment from a co-worker, or a compliment from a lover) are complex processes. As such, neuroscientists are still searching for the exact neural source and explanation of self-esteem and how it works—but don't despair! Here's what we do know. Through neuroimaging, and studies using innovative technology and machinery, we have identified several different networks of the brain, each with a distinct purpose or series of purposes. They control our emotional processing, valuation (of ourselves and others), theory of mind, memory, and learning—all of which tie into self-esteem!

The key structures that you need to know about are the hippocampus, the prefrontal cortex (PFC) and the cingulate cortex.

Our hippocampus, which handles our memory processes, forms the foundation of our self-worth. We draw upon our recollections and past experiences to try and gather (what our brain thinks) is valuable information about our current situation—even if that information is no longer helpful or useful! Remember the analogy of the mugger?

Here's another example. Say a school bully once pushed you into a shallow stream, causing you to choke and splutter and believe that you were drowning. Well, even as a grown adult who may since have learned how to swim, your brain might still attempt to 'help' you by creating a fear of water—because it associates water with that traumatic memory, and wants to protect you from experiencing that terror, shame, and confusion ever again. This can happen even if, logically, you know that you're in no real danger! That's the power of the brain, and specifically, of the hippocampus. You can probably see how this might once have been beneficial to our ancestors—they learned what predators to avoid, which plants were safe to eat, where was safe to set up a homestead, and that touching your hand to a burning flame is painful! Your hippocampus stores all of this and dishes it out when it feels that the situation calls for it—even when that information is no longer immediately or logically relevant.

Our working memory is a very involved process. It continually self-updates, meaning your hippocampus is always in action!

Another part of our brains that can affect self-esteem is the cingulate cortex. This structure is integrative, meaning it links together several other important structures of the brain, functioning almost like a bridge if you will. The cingulate cortex regulates our theory of mind. Basically, this means that it 'lights up' when we attempt to understand how others view us. This is essential for empathy and bonding, but it can be a real pain when we feel we aren't liked or valued by the important people in our life! As you can see, it's a bit of a double-edged sword. As you might have guessed, this is related to our self-perception or sense of self and can therefore have a big impact on self-esteem.

The pre-frontal cortex is the planning and organizing part of our brains. It is also responsible for analysis and evaluation. How often have you sat down after a social situation and thought back to the group's response when you made that joke that didn't quite land? That's your hippocampus (remembering), your cingulate cortex (bridging), and your PFC (analyzing and evaluating)—all working in tandem to influence your self-esteem. This can be a gift or a curse, depending on what we make of it.

That's where Cognitive Behavioral Therapy comes in.

Cognitive Behavioral Therapy or CBT is based on the currently accepted school of thought that our thoughts, feelings, physical sensations, and actions are all intimately tied to one another. Imagine them as points in a circle, affecting the others in all directions. Put simply, negative emotion or thought can make you feel physically ill, and a positive physical sensation can improve your mental state.

Have you ever noticed what you considered to be a flaw in the mirror, or received some negative professional feedback, or had a loved one hurt your feelings... and felt yourself spiralling? Do your thoughts fall into a pattern that goes something like "*I* failed, *I'm* ugly, *I'm* useless, *I'm* hated by this person..." etc.? If this happens, you are assigning a fixed and permanent value of self to a passing event, which is incorrect and illogical. The professional feedback is, by its nature, not personal (or it shouldn't be if you're dealing with mature professionals); the flaw you see in the mirror is a quirk that others find irresistible; the hurtful comment from your loved one is a reflection on them and their current mental state, not you as a person. CBT is designed to help interrupt these vicious shame spirals by catching and 'reprogramming' the negative thoughts before the obsessive circling can begin.

CBT differs from traditional psychoanalytic or talking therapy. Instead of digging into past traumas, it is designed to deal with and counter negative feelings that you're experiencing in the here and now. You're given specific exercises to help you recognize these patterns and 'undo' the damage of negative thinking. This doesn't mean letting people off the hook when it comes to accountability for their actions; it simply means recognizing that, while you are not responsible for the bad behaviours of others, you can control how you respond to them. CBT can help rewire your brain into the person you want to be.

CBT has been used to treat a wide range of symptoms and disorders, and in the past, it's helped women who have bipolar disorder, borderline personality disorder (BPD), eating disorders, anorexia, bulimia, obsessive-compulsive disorder (OCD), panic disorder, phobias, post-traumatic stress disorder (PTSD), psychosis, schizophrenia, sleep problems like insomnia, substance abuse, alcohol abuse, postpartum depression (PPD), seasonal affective disorder (SAD), depression, and anxiety. It may or may not be combined with medication, depending on what your GP or health team deem the most appropriate way of helping you.

If you find yourself frightened or put off by the previous paragraph, please don't think that I'm suggesting there's anything "broken" or "wrong" with you if you or anybody you know has been affected or touched by the listed problems or disorders; nor am I suggesting that anybody who would benefit from CBT is inherently 'crazy' (a derogatory term) or somehow 'less than' anybody else.

Many, many thousands of people a year seek out CBT or talking therapy as a preventative measure in the same way that it's advisable to go to your GP and dentist every so often for a check-up. In other situations, a person might be going through a particularly difficult event or transition—a break-up, a new career, a move, a bereavement—and benefit from an emotional 'tune-up' and a little extra attention to their thought processes during this more vulnerable period. It doesn't make you weak, fractured, or any less valid than anybody else. The world would be a much healthier place if everybody went to therapy!

Before signing up for a service or practitioner, be sure to do your research, and hold out for the right provider for you—somebody who aligns with your morals, beliefs, and goals.

Advantages of CBT, according to the NHS (2019):

- Cognitive Behavioral Therapy can be useful for patients for whom medicine alone, or other forms of therapy, haven't worked. Sometimes it can succeed as a supplement to, or in place of, these treatments (Hoffman, et al., 2012).
- It can be completed in a relatively short period when compared with other treatments and therapies: the usual treatment schedule takes place over roughly six weeks (Lorentzen, et al., 2020).
- Because CBT is highly structured, it is easily followed and very accessible, and available in a wide range of formats. This can include in-person therapy, online therapy, using guides and resources, and watching videos. There are even lots of apps and tools available, a list of which can be found on the NHS website.
- CBT involves strategies that will be beneficial to you throughout your entire life—not just through the period in which you're seeking therapy. These tools stay with you and will help you to regulate your emotions and handle conflict for the rest of your days.

Some Disadvantages of CBT, according to the NHS (2019):

- You get what you give: meaning that, if you're not fully invested in or committed to the process and the exercises, cognitive behavioural therapy will not work for you. While a therapist can advise you and teach you what you need to do, they cannot 'force' you through the process or do the work for you: responsibility rests on your shoulders.
- It may not be suitable for people with more complex mental disorders, as it requires a lot of structure.
- Through CBT, you will confront painful realities, hard truths, upsetting subject matter, and difficult emotions. You will look closely at themes and topics you may prefer to

avoid—just know that avoiding them isn't an effective long-term strategy, and confronting them with the help of a licensed professional is worth the initial discomfort it takes to overcome them once and for all.
- CBT is about YOU: it doesn't address systemic issues or the faults of other people in your life. CBT forces YOU to take accountability for what you can change and accept with grace and equanimity the things that you cannot. This may seem unfair or may seem to suggest that there is no justice in the world, but the inner peace that you learn by developing the ability to control your reactions is worth the hefty investment of time, money, and effort.

Overall, CBT can be an excellent tool in your self-care arsenal, helping you to challenge and replace negative thoughts you have about yourself. *You* can take control of your thoughts and feelings, which will improve your self-image and encourage you to believe in yourself. When you believe in yourself fully, you come to understand that failure is a part of the process and that setbacks are not the end of the world.

AFFIRMATIONS

Self-belief is vital for your happiness and success; it affects everything you do, from your personal life to your professional life to your inner world. The choices you make and the dreams you dream all come down to how you view yourself, how you measure your own value and worth as a human being, and how you assess and make use of your incredible potential. Self-belief is the key to creating the life you want to live.

SELF-BELIEF AFFIRMATIONS

- If I don't believe in myself, why should anyone else?
- Each day, I believe in myself more and more.
- Each day, I feel more powerful and capable.
- I believe in myself even if others do not.
- I see the potential in myself and take action to fulfil it.

AFFIRMATIONS TO BOOST YOUR CONFIDENCE

- I acknowledge my own self-worth; my self-confidence is rising.
- I am confident in who I am and my abilities.
- I am bold and strong.
- Confidence is like a muscle: the more I use it, the stronger I get.
- I boldly go after what I want in life.
- I confidently meet any challenge.
- Confidence empowers me to take action and live life to the fullest.
- Every step I take is proof of my courage and tenacity.
- My confidence commands respect and attention.

AFFIRMATIONS TO RAISE YOUR INNER VOICE

- I stand up for myself.
- I speak my mind with confidence.
- I express myself honestly.
- I can assert myself in any situation.
- I am allowed to say no to things that do not serve me or make me happy.
- My voice matters, my opinion counts, and so do others'.
- My voice is just as important as anyone else's.
- It is OK to ask for help when I need it.

AFFIRMATIONS FOR CHARISMA

- I bring warm energy to everyone I meet.
- People talk positively about me and enjoy being around me.
- I enjoy meeting and talking with new people.
- I always find something to talk about, my conversation flows.
- I enjoy finding out about other people.
- People feel safe talking to me.
- People love talking to me.
- I make people happy; I can make them laugh and enjoy themselves.
- People take my opinions seriously.
- I can inspire others with my words.

EXERCISE

Write down three negative thoughts, and then rewrite them using the principles of CBT we looked at in this chapter.

For example:

Thought: *"I'm a terrible mother because my son fell and grazed his knee."*

Rewritten thought: *"I am a loving mother, and I got distracted for a moment, and my son fell down. I comforted him, cleaned his grazed knee, and put a plaster on it. This one mistake does not detract from my worth as a parent overall."*

4
LEVEL UP YOUR CONFIDENCE

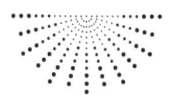

William James is famously quoted as saying that "most people live in a restricted circle of potential." But what exactly does this restricted circle mean? Is it externally or internally imposed? As you will have gathered from the previous chapters in this book, the answer is a little bit of both.

If somebody in this world doesn't reach their full potential, it's often not the case that they lack ambition, intelligence, resources, or opportunity: in fact, it's very possible to underestimate or undersell yourself, even if or when you have these various factors working in your favour. Why is that, you might be wondering? Well, that's the question this chapter aims to answer. We're going to take a deeper look at self-confidence and self-esteem, and debunk the common myth that these are traits you're simply born with (or traits that you acquire alongside good fortune, career advancement, or through relationships; realistically, if you don't have confidence in yourself, none of these factors will magically manifest it).

Many people who don't live up to their potential do so because of a lack of self-confidence or self-esteem. If you're reading this and thinking, "But I know that I have no, or very little, self-esteem—that's why I'm reading this book! So, am I doomed to failure?" Please don't panic! Just as self-esteem is not an accident of birth or a prize that's awarded for societally-recognized milestones of 'success' (itself a very dubious, fluid, and personal concept!), it is *also not a fixed attribute*. Having low or no self-confidence or self-esteem at one point in your life does not mean that you will never be able to attain or enjoy it. Remember the previous chapter, in which we looked at neuroplasticity and just how amazing and adaptable the biological make-up of our brains can be? Confidence and self-esteem are extremely malleable and changeable. They *can be achieved over time* through the power of positive actions and self-affirmations.

CONFIDENCE STEPS

- I WON'T DO IT
- I CAN'T DO IT
- I WANT TO DO IT
- HOW DO I DO IT?
- I'LL TRY TO DO IT
- I CAN DO IT
- I WILL DO IT
- YES, I DID IT!

Put another way, confidence doesn't have its roots in our *actual* ability to do a certain thing or maintain a certain relationship: rather, it is our *perceived ability* to do so. This is a fancier way of saying that old aphorism we've all heard, which has its basis in real wisdom—fake it till you make it!

Below are some examples of this. Self-confidence and self-esteem are dependent, not on your *actual* ability to do the following, but on your *belief* in your ability to do them:

. . .

1. Public Speaking or Performing

This could mean presenting during a big conference call, participating in a dance recital, arguing in a publicized debate, acting, singing, or dancing in a production of your favourite musical or play, or making a speech in aid of your favourite political or charitable cause. If you worry that you're going to forget your lines, fluff a step, trip over your words, omit an important piece of data, or spend the entire time frozen or trembling in fright—*but then get up and do it anyway*—believe it or not, you are on your way to building true confidence or self-esteem.

Feeling the fear and doing it anyway is a sure-fire way to begin working the muscle of self-confidence. It is an act of radical bravery to ignore your inner critic and do the very thing you feel you 'can't' do. In some contexts, this is also called exposure therapy. You will realize that not only did you successfully overcome your fear, but you also didn't suffer any horrible adverse consequences; this makes you more willing to get out there and do it again, and it's exactly how you create a chain reaction (or series of building blocks) towards a more liberated future.

2. Leading a Team

Many women in positions of leadership, even when they've worked hard to get there, can suffer from imposter syndrome or self-doubt when they're given a team to manage. This could mean managing a department (or the whole company) at work, coaching a sports team, teaching a class at your local recreational centre, or running a household for your family (which takes an immense amount of time management, organization, administration, budgeting, people skills, and energy).

CEOs, mothers, athletes, and educators alike sometimes feel that they've somehow 'bluffed' their way into leadership—as if they're faking it and have manipulated or fooled everyone around them into believing that they're competent. Such people wait for the sword dangling over their head to come crashing down and have their grand lie revealed to the world at large. I'm using hyperbolic language here to demonstrate how these anxious thoughts can run away with us, spiralling out of control and dragging us into whirlpools of self-doubt.

If you're a woman who looks at the people over whom you have some sort of control and worries about whether you're doing right by them, you may be suffering from low self-confidence or self-esteem. But don't despair. This means that you are taking your role seriously and proceeding with integrity and goodwill: the very fact that you're asking yourself, "Am I good enough?" in nine out of ten cases means that you are.

After all, how many corrupt or power-hungry business people with selfish motivations ever wonder, "Am I a qualified and fair authority figure?" How many abusive or neglectful parents take the time to sit in introspection and self-examination, asking, "Am I creating a life of compassion, order, boundaries, love, and safety for my children?" The very fact that you *care about the people you're leading* most likely means that you already have everything it takes to be the best possible leader you can be. It's unlikely you would be in this position in the first place if you weren't—positions of authority aren't handed out as favours; they're usually given to qualified and caring, competent leaders.

But if you still feel like you're undeserving of your role, this chapter, and this book, can help.

3. Handling Conflict

"Happy wife, happy life" is not the formula for long-lasting, blissful relationships that some claim it to be. Of course, you should be, and deserve to be, happy, peaceful, and content the majority of the time, but a relationship *entirely lacking conflict*—whether it's romantic, friendly, familial, or professional—is not healthy. This is because it usually means that at least one party is stifling their true feelings, desires, or irritations.

Thinking of the people whom you love and cherish most in the world, can you honestly claim that those relationships have never endured a single second of irritation, frustration, miscommunication, sadness, anger, betrayal, or priorities that simply didn't line up? Conflict is not only inevitable, but I truly believe it is necessary if we wish to proceed in love and light with honesty, self-awareness, and a deeper understanding of those with whom we choose to share our lives.

Conflict resolution, and what, for lack of a better phrase, I'll call "compassionate arguing," are essential life skills, but many of us do not grow up with ideal models for tackling problems and overcoming obstacles. We witness people in our lives name-calling, going for the jugular, and going "off-topic" during what should have been frank but loving discussions: a talk that should have been about the neglected piles of dishes in the sink becomes an attack on the guilty party's personality, rather than the issue at hand: "You're lazy, you're irresponsible, you don't care about my feelings," etc. Notice how these statements don't criticize the action (the unwashed dishes) but the person? How do you think that makes them feel? Lousy, right? And certainly unwilling to do the dishes in the future, considering you've made it clear you think so lowly of them.

Now imagine the result if, instead of those statements (which wrongly made blanket assertions about the person as a whole), you replaced them with a model referred to in therapeutic circles as "when you/ I feel." If it's not clear what I mean by this, I'll give an example. "When you don't do the dishes, I feel as if you don't take my requests or comfort seriously."

Can you see how that shifts the onus from the neglectful (non)dishwasher to the person making the statement, who is not hiding their feelings but is taking responsibility for the way they receive the other's actions? This communicates the true root of their feelings (after all, this issue is clearly not about the dishes but a pattern of disregard) and gives the offending party a much better shot at seeing the reality of the problem and addressing it.

Here are some more examples:

"When you cancel our plans at the last minute, I feel as if you don't value my time or the time we spend together."

"When you called my crafting business a 'little hobby,' it sounded patronizing, and I felt as if you don't believe in my ability or respect my skills and acumen."

"When you said you didn't like my new haircut, I felt unattractive to you, and that made me sad."

Of course, there are a million books about conflict resolution out there, and I sadly don't have the space, in this book, to go over other techniques, but when you use these little tips and tricks to assert yourself and your boundaries, without triggering the ingrained defence mechanisms of others (who might otherwise not truly 'hear' you or be willing to have an open and passionate discussion), you will find your confidence growing by the bucketload.

If you're somebody who has not grown up with unconditional positive regard, you may be afraid that others will withdraw their love or respect if you express a complaint or a need. First of all, I promise you that nobody deserving of your love will withdraw their own in response to a respectfully drawn boundary or conversation. Secondly, it's okay if you currently lack the confidence to do this: this book, and these affirmations, will help you get there.

. . .

4. Big Life Changes

Whether it's leaving home, moving house (or country!), starting (or going back to!) school, embarking on a new career, taking the plunge and committing to a new relationship, or finding the courage to leave an existing one that's become toxic, people sometimes feel afraid to make big life changes. After all, doing so is betting on yourself, and when you have little or no self-confidence or self-esteem, that can seem impossible. Believing that you can do so is the very first step—and I'm here to help.

It's a long-held and established truth that the beliefs we hold—whether or not they are factually accurate—can have a real influence on the shape of our lives and our chosen course of action. As you now know, our understanding of neuroplasticity reveals that we can rewire our brains and influence the direction of our thoughts. This means that even if you've previously stifled your inner light, been timid, non-combative, or afraid to assert yourself and ask for—no, demand!—what you need, this is *possible to change*.

Self-confidence and self-esteem are *volitional*. This is another way of saying, "by choice." That's why I keep referring to them as muscles—they become stronger over time through frequent use! Just like learning to read, riding a bike, or running a marathon, a skill that you may have struggled with when you first began will soon become as automatic and second-nature as breathing.

"Yes, yes," I hear you saying. "But surely it isn't all down to me? Confidence *is* affected by external circumstances, too, isn't it?"

You're correct. Our self-confidence and self-esteem, like our overall fitness level, can wax, wane, and alter throughout a lifetime. Of course, your confidence is going to take a hit if you experience the loss of a job, or a painful divorce, or an eviction, or the loss of a family member. Humans are social creatures that crave approval and stability, and when these are threatened, our first instinct is often to look within to find the 'flaw' there that's responsible. Because after all, if we identify it (and, in doing so, criticize ourselves), we can stop the bad thing from happening again, right?

"I was a bad wife, so it's no wonder she wanted to leave me."

"I wouldn't have lost my home if I was more professionally successful. I'm a failure."

"I wasn't there enough for my mom, and that's why she was injured."

It's a way of coping with the tragedy and trying to avoid a repeat. But it is based on emotion, not logic. Now, I want to be clear that neither emotion nor logic is inherently or by definition either good or bad. What we chose to apply to our responses has an impact on us.

Using the techniques in the previous chapter, we can replace the thoughts I've just listed with the following, respectively.

"The divorce came about because of complicated and personal factors: I may not have been a perfect wife, and I will work hard to identify and address my flaws for my next relationship. I am not solely to blame for this sad circumstance, and nor am I a bad person just because this relationship wasn't meant to be."

"I try hard in my career and have been actively applying for better-paying jobs or an internal promotion. The fact that I am not currently paid enough to keep my house is not a reflection of my abilities or my moral worth. It is just a sad and difficult reality of capitalism."

"Even if I had been with my mum when she fell, I would not have been able to prevent the injury. I would have called emergency services, just as the people around her did at the time. Her being hurt has nothing to do with my absence or presence. However, I can resolve to see her more often and strengthen our relationship in the future."

Notice how these responses take accountability and identify things that the thinker wants to change without branding them as a terrible or irredeemable person or forcing them to take the *entire* brunt of the situation on their shoulders?

Believe it or not, these are actually affirmations! Yes, they are extremely specific to the thinker's situation, but they uplift the positive and identify what needs to change without castigating, belittling, or dismissing the person. In challenging situations like the ones above, we *all* deserve compassion and a nuanced, logical understanding of what happened. This *must* start from within.

So, what tangible steps can you take to build your confidence?

TAKE RISKS AND BUILD ENDURANCE

This is the "fake it till you make it" philosophy we spoke about earlier. If you can slowly expose yourself (in a safe way) to things that frighten you, you can build up your resilience and feel more confident tackling them in the future.

If you're worried about your ability to be a good parent, why not babysit your friend's kids for a night? If you think you are not 'smart enough,' why not join a night class or a book club that stretches your horizons and pushes your boundaries? (Though I promise you, you're smart enough as you are.) If you are scared to get back on the dating scene, why not commit yourself to going for a coffee with someone your friends pick out for you or help you find? You could even put a timer on it by scheduling a relaxing event, like a massage or a haircut, afterwards. If you get through those twenty minutes, or however long you set aside, you will realize that meeting new people is not as frightening as it seemed, and more willing to try out longer dates in the future!

The trick is to create *small, tangible, achievable* milestones that will help you achieve momentum and recognize your progress. Avoid doing too much, too fast—this has more potential to go wrong, which could damage your confidence instead of building it up. Slow and steady wins the race!

HAVE FUN WITH POWER POSES!

Power poses are not pseudoscience—they've been proven to work (Elsesser, 2018)! You may feel silly at first, but try standing in front of a mirror and placing your hands on your hips. Widen your shoulders. Stand tall. Lift your chin. Give your biggest smile.

Our bodies notoriously have difficulty separating cause from effect—a phenomenon you can use to your advantage! If your posture is confident, happy, and strong, this actually tricks your brain into thinking you feel the same way! And the same is true the other way around: if you slouch, whisper, look aside, anxiously fidget or crack your fingers or play with your hair, this will *tell your brain that you are afraid, nervous, or not feeling confident.* Isn't that remarkable? In a way, this tip comes under the same 'law' as the previous one: by physically arranging your body in a confident way and moving with confidence, your self-esteem will grow. Try it out!

Draw inspiration from others. Do you have a family member, friend, colleague, or even a celebrity whom you admire, look up to, and wish to emulate? Are you envious of their confidence? Well, good news—you can simply steal it for yourself! I'm being tongue in cheek, of course, and you should never endeavour to be anybody but yourself (since you are good enough as you are)—but if there is somebody in your life who is particularly confident, try to channel their energy in moments when you doubt yourself. Ask, "How would they react to this situation?" and see if imitating their posture, tone, or passion helps boost your self-esteem. (Soon, this will become automatic, and you won't need to look to others—you'll have confidence in yourself!)

BE GOAL-ORIENTED

If a conversation or task intimidates you, focus on what it will achieve and the positivity it will bring into your life. If you're scared to go back to school, visualize the benefits of your new and exciting enhanced education. Will it help you get on the career track of your dreams? Will you build meaningful and invigorating relationships with your peers and teachers, who share your goals and passion? Will it add structure, meaning, and purpose to your days and years? Similarly, if you're afraid to give a speech for a cause about which you're passionate, visualize the extra donations or activism your speech will incite and concentrate on the greater good and the higher goal. Often, reminding ourselves *why* we are doing something can give us that boost to get through something that makes us nervous.

Have a practice run! Even if this is just in the privacy of your own head. It's related to the visualization mentioned in the previous tip. If you are performing in a dance recital, go through your routine in your mind (and not just during normal, physical rehearsals) during quiet moments. When the big night comes, you'll feel more confident knowing that you've drilled and drilled yourself on each step.

This is also an example of manifestation: if you picture yourself nailing the routine over and over, you're well on your way to actually making it happen and creating a self-fulfilling prophecy! The same is also true of negative catastrophizing, so don't dwell on anxious visions of yourself falling or making a misstep—just let those bad thoughts float away, like dandelion fluff on the breeze. Say, "I see you, bad thought, but I don't care." Simple but effective!

MORE FORMULAS FOR GROWING YOUR SELF-CONFIDENCE AND SELF-ESTEEM

If you've read this far, but you're still having some difficulty coming up with practical, tangible exercises to increase your self-confidence and self-esteem, don't worry—this chapter includes several more exercises for you:

1. Identify and Challenge Self-Limiting Beliefs—then Change the Narrative!

This has been touched on or hinted at throughout this chapter already, but I'll make it more concrete here, beneath this subheading: if you can dig down deep, all the way into the workings of your mind, and find the beliefs that limit you, you can then work to consciously challenge them and change the narrative of your life.

For example, if, after some self-examination, you find that you believe you are 'bad' at golfing, crocheting, playing football, or swimming, actively challenging these beliefs through affirmations and exposure to the activities will grow your confidence.

Practice! Practice! Practice! Grow the muscle! Train your mind. Do it all over again. Again and again, until you make it perfect—if you wanna make it perfect. I want to warn you though that aiming for perfection is as dangerous as a vice. Just be good at it, just be better at it, better than your previous unsatisfactory self, compete with yourself, not with others, please yourself, not others. Over time, this will rewrite your thought patterns, your belief in your own abilities, and the overall trajectory of your life.

2. Own Your Achievements

Sadly, studies have shown that women are quick to demur when their successes are mentioned: they will credit the investment, time, efforts, and good qualities of others before they are likely to praise themselves or take credit for a job well done (Steiger, 2013). Men have been proven to do the opposite: they have no problem taking credit for their own perceived talent, intelligence, or acumen—they have been conditioned to feel entitled to success, whereas women have been conditioned to feel that they don't deserve it (ibid.).

This infuriating fact is a result of millennia of patriarchy and toxic masculinity, which harms everyone in the long run. Women don't apply for the pay raises, promotions, projects, or positions for which they're more than qualified, and men end up out of their depth in roles for which they don't have the acumen because of this phenomenon (Ludden, 2011).

So, knowing this, why do we, as enlightened women and feminists, fall into this pattern? Well, because it's often not a conscious decision. It's not always as if we think, in such explicit terms, "a man is better qualified for this than me." It's often the unconscious result of conditioning that has trained us to be demure, modest, and submissive. We are taught that if we don't embody these qualities, we are less feminine: therefore, it is 'unseemly' to seem to take pride in our own accomplishments. Even as children, we play down our accomplishments because we don't want to stand out from the other girls suffering under the very same conditioning! Internalized misogyny even pits women against women, and some insecure women baulk at the idea of another woman being successful because of this harmful messaging, of which everybody eventually ends up the victim. We are taught not to be competitive or boastful when the same traits are glorified in men from birth.

Culture also has a strong impact on this. Collectivist cultures (those spanning the Middle East, Asia, and Africa, for example) value modesty in social interactions. People in these cultures are taught to downplay their individual successes and celebrate and uplift those of others.

So how can you combat this tendency if you've found yourself doing it? Well, one thing I might suggest is creating literal documentation of your highlight moments! Get creative with this. You could make a list, a journal, a chart, a mind-map, a comic book, a painting, or even compose a song! Embrace your inner creativity in a way that shines a light on the best and brightest moments of your life so far—for which you and you alone have been responsible!

3. Contain Your Failures

The inverse of the previous is also, sadly, true. Women are less likely to take credit for their successes than men are, but they are quicker to take ownership of perceived or actual failure (Haynes & Lawrence, 2012).

Women are more likely to believe that they did not succeed in a task or a relationship because of their own intrinsic lack of capability, intellect, effort, or validity (Kay & Shipman, 2014). Men, on the other hand, are far more likely to blame external factors for their failure, citing the task's difficulty, or their team's incompetence, or their boss's attitude, or their tools, or the timeline in which they were meant to complete the task (ibid.). Also, men have more of a tendency to categorize the failure as a single, isolated incident, whereas women approach the failure more globally: that is, they use it as an opportunity for introspection to evaluate their skills overall (ibid.). This can lead to women thinking, "I failed in this regard; it's because I'm under-qualified/unintelligent/unmotivated/a bad leader overall."

This has a supreme impact on self-confidence and self-worth. Therefore, any opportunity that presents even the possibility of failure can be very threatening to a woman's self-confidence, self-worth, and self-regard! This means that, compared to men, women are less likely to take professional risks or subject themselves to the possibility of failure.

This is called an "attribution habit," and it can be extremely powerful. Because of their strength, I advise you to take time for an honest assessment of *both the internal and external factors* that may have played a part in the failure. You'll realize that it was not entirely your fault, which is essential for growing self-confidence and self-esteem.

4. Identify Role Models

Examine what it is about the role models that you admire. Do you respect their conflict resolution skills? Their ambition? Their creativity? Their compassion? Their emotional regulation? Their empathy? Their competency in the workplace?

Take this way down to a micro-level, too, if you're so inclined: do you like the way they do their winged eyeliner or the way they meal-plan every Sunday? Do you like their insightful blog or their cooking abilities? Their ability to build and run a removal company from the ground up?

Whatever it is, ask yourself if those are habits or traits you'd like to attempt to incorporate into your own lifestyle. *Don't copy,* but honour and celebrate them in your own little rituals (in a way that won't make them uncomfortable, of course); there's nothing wrong with borrowing a little piece of somebody you admire to help you feel better about yourself—provided you remember that you were always enough, to begin with, and use this only as a way of giving yourself a little boost. After all, that little boost can make a big change and help you achieve huge things!

GROWTH MINDSET

It is essential that you employ a growth mindset versus a fixed mindset. But what are these?

A growth mindset can be defined as one oriented towards evolution and positive change. A growth mindset says, "failure and challenges provide me with a chance to grow. I have the ability to study my interests and grow my knowledge base. Feedback makes me stronger and better. I take inspiration from the successes of others. I enjoy new things, even if I am not immediately brilliant at them."

In contrast, a fixed mindset says, "failure is indicative of my worth as a whole, and means that I am universally and irrevocably incompetent. I apply black and white, binary thinking. I am either good at something, or I am not, with no ability to change. Being challenged is unpleasant and proves my lack of worth. My potential is already predetermined and cannot be changed. Frustrations and obstacles mean I should give up and stop trying. Feedback and criticism are always personal, and the people giving it dislike or hate me; they believe my work is fully worthless if they make one negative comment. It is safer to stick with what I know."

A fixed mindset means that you never step outside of your comfort zone, never challenge your internalized beliefs, and as a consequence of this, never expand your horizons or reach your potential. Adapting to challenges and feedback can be tough, but employing a growth mindset will expand your pathways and abilities (as well as your self-confidence and self-esteem) exponentially.

WOMEN AND CONFIDENCE IN THE WORKPLACE

Research conducted by the University of Glasgow, in conjunction with My Confidence Matters, found that an astonishing 75% of women reported a lack of confidence in the workplace (Perriam, 2017). The survey, which collected data from over 300 employed women in a wide range of sectors and industries, found that of those who had taken a career break (for child-care, personal development, their health, or other reasons), 62% felt less confident upon their return to the workplace (ibid.).

Similarly, one of the most commonly reported situations in which women lack confidence is when asking for a raise, asking for a promotion, or (if they're a business owner or freelancer) increasing their prices. 43% of women interviewed reported feeling uncomfortable doing so, or even 'unworthy,' as if they were somehow undeserving of payment and benefits commensurate with their ever-expanding skills and experience (ibid.).

A further 40% reported feeling uncomfortable and lacking confidence when required to make a presentation or a speech (ibid.). This isn't surprising, considering how internalized misogyny and sexism can lead women to self-censor, or be spoken over, interrupted, or dismissed in traditionally male-dominated environments.

34% of women reported feeling intimidated by their colleagues or boss (ibid.). Harassment and bullying towards women proliferate on both a systemic and microscopic level, and many workplaces don't have appropriate structures in place to protect employees from inappropriate behaviour, unwanted sexual advances, dehumanizing or objectifying comments, or degradation. Men are also victims of this type of abuse, and the patriarchal acceptance of it harms everyone.

But intimidation can also be more subtle than overt cruelty. Women, in particular, can sometimes feel that they will never match up to the success of others. They see others promoted ahead of them or praised and imagine that their work could never reach such a laudable standard—because women are socialized to lack confidence. 27% of women interviewed reported feeling a lack of confidence when competing with work colleagues, and 19% were uncomfortable chairing a meeting (ibid.).

Geraldine Perriam, a research associate of the University of Glasgow, explains this phenomenon thusly (ibid.):

"It is not, and should not be, a given that women experience low levels of confidence due to their gender. Masculinist 'norms' that are weighted towards specific, established types of organizational structure and demands on employees have been demonstrated to undermine women's self-confidence."

One of the most significant and exciting findings of this survey was that 57% of women said they would be interested in entering a community of like-minded individuals centred on boosting confidence and empowering women in the workplace (ibid.). This indicates a very real demand for books such as this one, and if you're one of those women hoping to boost your confidence in the workplace, the good news is that you already hold the solution in your hands!

I ♥ AFFIRMATIONS

AFFIRMATIONS

- I speak my mind with confidence.
- I assert my boundaries and my voice.
- I do not allow myself to be silenced.
- I speak up loud and proud.
- I do not allow myself to be patronized.
- I own my womanhood and my skills as a leader.
- I do not allow myself to be harassed.
- I am a competent professional who deserves to be treated as such.
- I do not allow myself to self-censor.
- My opinions are valid, welcome, and useful.
- Men are not more entitled to success than me.

- Other women are not my enemy.
- Other women are not in competition with me.
- I am not in competition with other women.
- I will help others 'up the ladder' behind me.
- I will lead with compassion and emotional insight.
- I have all the necessary skills and resilience to reach my full potential.
- I hunger for knowledge and personal growth.
- I am always evolving and getting closer to the best possible version of "me."
- I am outgoing. I am taking active steps to overcome my shyness. I am relaxed, easy-going, and social.
- I am confident when meeting new people.
- Sharing my thoughts and feelings is easy for me.
- I am confident and relaxed when talking to the opposite sex.
- I am comfortable socializing with strangers.
- I am confident, positive, warm, and friendly.
- I radiate ease and self-assurance.
- I will overcome my shyness.
- I will make positive connections with others.
- Other people want to connect with me.
- I have valuable input to give.
- I bring a lot to the table.
- I will have a full and exciting social life.
- I give off positive energy to others.
- Socializing and meeting new people make me happy.
- I am worthy of romance, professional success, and a fulfilling family life.
- I am capable of achieving whatever I put my mind to.
- I don't have to 'choose' between options—I can have it all!

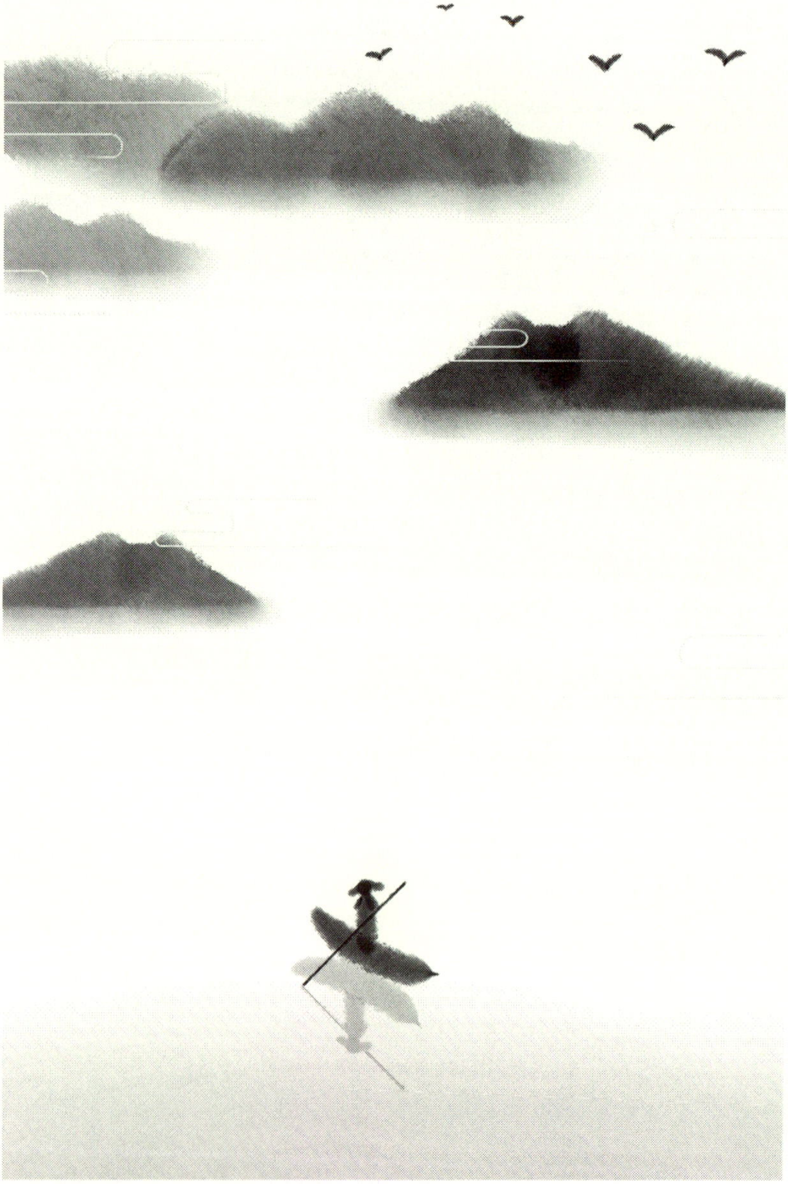

EXERCISE

Write down five things you would like to change about your life, and then two things you need to do in order to implement these changes. Use the formula, "I would like to change…" followed by, "I could change this if…"

For example:

I would like to change the way I'm belittled and patronized at work.

I could change this if… *I learned to advocate for myself and speak up against mistreatment.*

I could change this if… *I acknowledged the worth I bring to the workplace and found another job with a less hostile company.*

5
RAISE YOUR INNER VOICE

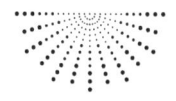

You deserve to take up more space.

Notice my use of the word 'more' in that sentence. You might be thinking, "I'm already good at asserting my boundaries and standing up for myself; I'm already skilled at identifying, defending, and reaching my goals." If that sounds like you, I'm sincerely happy for you and proud of you, and I hope your personal and spiritual growth continues to grow exponentially!

The thing is, subtle misogyny, whether internalized or external, can sometimes lead some, not all, women to believe that they are taking up 'enough' space—or even more than their fair share!—when in reality, they still move through the world actively making themselves smaller, quieter, more amenable and conciliatory because they have been socialized to believe that this is what a polite and conscientious person does.

Please don't think I'm advocating for rudeness, selfishness, or confrontation. I'm merely attempting to highlight a phenomenon in which women are often told to *make way and make space for others in this world,* while men are socialized to believe they are *entitled to that space.* The reality is that you, as a woman, are just entitled to that space as him.

Consider the phenomenon of 'manspreading.' Seems innocuous, right? If you're unfamiliar with the term, it's a word used to describe when a man, usually on public transport, spreads his legs wide, often allowing them to spread beyond the confines of his assigned or taken seat and spilling out over onto or beyond the next. This either prevents other people from sitting in the seat beside him or, if somebody is occupying that seat, it means that person has to make themselves smaller (by drawing their knees and elbows close together and sitting in an uncomfortable position) throughout the journey.

In this scenario, the person manspreading—the phenomenon is named after a man, because while women are obviously also capable of doing so, men, having been socialized to be less considerate than women, are the most frequent offenders—have *prioritized their own comfort over the comfort of the person beside them.* Somebody else on that bus, or train carriage, may even have to stand throughout the journey because they don't feel comfortable asking the person manspreading to stop doing so.

This is an example of how, historically, men are taught to occupy space, physically and emotionally, more than we women are. Am I suggesting you go about your day making other commuters' lives miserable? Of course not! I'm using this anecdote to suggest that there are ways in which you are probably literally and emotionally shrinking your presence—ways you may not even realize!

So. Even if you feel you occupy 'enough' space, I'm here to tell you to take more. Raise your voice when speaking. Don't allow yourself to be spoken over or spoken down to. Assert your right to boundaries, to love, to respect, to honesty, to that promotion, to that passion project that's been burning away in your heart but which you've never dared to pursue until now.

Ask yourself, "Would a rich, white, straight man hesitate to ask for this?"

If the answer is no, grant yourself the same privileges that the demographic has come to expect. You deserve them just as much, if not more.

In this chapter, we'll look at several topics. First, we'll investigate the idea of assertiveness: its definition, what exactly it means, how you can embody it, and how to bring it into your everyday interactions, large and small. Secondly, we'll look at shyness and social phobias. What causes them? How do they affect us? How can we overcome them? How do we dare to imagine just how beautiful our lives can be, once we are no longer burdened by them? Thirdly, we'll look at communication. What constitutes good communication? How do we better advocate for ourselves and others in the way that we interact with the world around us? And of course, as always, at the end of this chapter, you'll find a bountiful list of positive affirmations that you can incorporate into your daily routine in order to raise your inner voice, take up more space, overcome shyness and social phobias, and communicate in a healthy way.

With that established, let's jump in!

ASSERTIVENESS: WHY YOU DESERVE TO OCCUPY SPACE

Many things lead us to believe that we don't deserve to occupy space. I know that in the past when my confidence has been at its lowest due to break-ups, perceived professional failures, and setbacks to my lifestyle due to unexpected changes—not to mention cruel comments from, or arguments with, friends or family that claimed to love me—I have found it extremely difficult to consider myself "worthy" of space. I would think to myself that these instances reflected an inherent flaw in me: that I was unlovable, or a bad employee, or simply not trying hard enough. I blamed my lack of resilience for what I thought was my weakness, not realizing that my emotions were merely a natural and healthy response to adverse circumstances. In those moments, I didn't feel that my true self was worthy of being seen, that my opinions and dreams were worthy of being heard, that my beauty could ever exist in the eye of the beholder—because I couldn't see it in myself.

But the truth is that I, like others, and like you—yes, you, with this book in your hand—am just as worthy as anybody else. We all deserve to be seen and heard as our authentic selves. We deserve to take care of our own needs, and not just the needs of others. We deserve to nurture our hopes and dreams as if they are beautiful gardens of scented flowers and nourishing fruits—not weeds to be ripped up from their roots or trampled cruelly, unceremoniously underfoot.

How did I begin to realize this? Well, have you ever been discussing a problem or a source of personal pain with a friend or loved one, only to hear yourself saying some variation of "I'm sorry, I'm talking too much," or "I'm sorry, I'm being annoying," or even, "I'm sorry, I'll shut up now?"

This is the language we fall back on when we don't feel as if the inner workings of our souls are valid or worth bringing to the attention of others—even people who we know love us and care for us! We trick ourselves into thinking that we only exist to listen, to console, to provide solutions and answers and amends: never to talk, to be consoled, to ask for those same solutions and answers and amends. But that isn't fair. It isn't fair on us, and it isn't fair on our friends and loved ones who *actually want* to be there for us and listen to the turmoil of our hearts! Studies have shown that people actually feel more valued, loved, and respected *when we allow them to help us with our problems.* By never asking for help or taking up space, by mitigating yourself with the statements I listed in the last paragraph, you are actually creating a one-sided dynamic in which you don't allow your loved ones to provide the same solace that you provide for them. Relationships cannot always be 50/50—sometimes they tip to 80/20 when one person is in need, and that is perfectly okay. In a healthy relationship, that balance will right itself and swing back around eventually.

What I've just described is a form of over-apologizing. A subtler form of this is the mitigating and softening that a lot of women use in their everyday language, especially in formal or professional communications. Have you ever found yourself using phrases like, "sorry to bother you," "I was just wondering," or "if it's not too much trouble," and "no worries if not" (sometimes with an obscene number of exclamation marks to drive the point home…)?

If so, you're not alone. A lot of women, when making a reasonable statement or request (like reminding somebody of a company policy or asking for a document to be signed) have been socialized to feel bad about making this "demand," and will therefore attempt to soften it with language like the phrases I listed in the previous paragraph. In many cases, a man faced with the same task would feel no need to adjust his tone; thus, he would simply make the statement or ask the question. He has not been raised to question whether he has a 'right' to do so without being perceived as 'bossy' or a 'shrew' or 'uncompromising.' If you have noticed yourself doing this, it could be an indicator that you are uncomfortable taking up the space you deserve. The next time you have to write a text or an email like this or even make such a request in person, try it without any softening language. It might feel odd at first, but you are not being rude by doing your job, or by making an everyday request or asking a question!

Saying 'no' and failing to protect our time and resources can also be a big indicator that we are uncomfortable taking up the space we deserve.

Has this ever happened to you?

You're in the middle of a big project at work, raising children, preparing for your in-laws to visit at the weekend, and caring for your elderly parents… when a friend asks you to help them move house next week.

"Of course!" you exclaim, blithely, almost without thinking, a smile plastered wide on your face. Internally, you're screaming, crying. Your body is bruised and exhausted, and emotionally you're at your wits' end. But you can't leave your friend without help, right? That would be cruel and heartless, wouldn't it?

Well, actually… no, it wouldn't.

And hey, don't feel bad if you've been there—I've been guilty of this in the past, too. When we love people, and we try to move through the world being a good person, we end up saying 'yes' to a lot of things, whether it's out of ambition, a desire to be liked, a need to be busy, or simply not wanting to let anybody down—it can sometimes be really difficult to say 'no.' But 'no' is not a dirty word. 'No' does not need qualifying, explaining, or apologizing for. Repeat this after me: 'No' is a complete sentence.

"Can I buy you a drink?"

"No."

"Will you watch my kids on Saturday?"

"No."

"Will you drive me to the airport this weekend?"

"No."

"Jan's out sick—will you take on her workload until she comes back?"

"No."

"I know you said you're not in the mood, but can we have sex?"

"No."

"Can you wear more make-up to look more professional?"

"No."

"No" really is a magic word—try it, and revel in its power! It can feel very uncomfortable, at first, to firmly and unapologetically reject a person's advances, request for a favour, or attempt to trample over your boundaries, but remember that *you are the guardian of your time and resources.* Nobody is as invested in protecting them as you are, and if you don't defend and hoard them, nobody else will even attempt to.

It does not make you a bad partner to not want sex. It does not make you a bad friend if you're unable to help somebody move house. It does not make you a bad employee if you're unwilling to pick up another's slack. And it does not make you a bad parent to be the 'bad guy' sometimes, denying your kids things or activities that could be harmful to them.

Taking up space means protecting your time with the power of your "no." Do you want the time, space, and money to write your novel finally? To take up kickboxing? To learn to embroider? To backpack through South America? Carve that time with the mighty sword of your "no," and feel no guilt for doing so. I hereby absolve you! You are a person with your own ambitions, dreams, and interests, in addition to being a partner, a friend, an employee, a parent, or a daughter—it is important to occupy space by advocating for yourself outside of and beyond these identities. Who is the woman beyond the labels? Take a moment to investigate her and think about what you can do to bring her into the spotlight she deserves.

Realize, also, that your thoughts and contributions can enlighten and elevate a conversation. You are not required to sit silently in the corner, answering questions only when spoken to like a scorned child. People are eager to hear your opinions and anecdotes, so share them loudly and proudly! This will foster deeper connections and help you to forge new ones.

On a related note, it's okay to be vulnerable with people around you. There is nothing embarrassing or annoying about sharing your fears and insecurities—in fact, this has helped me to create some of the closest and longest-lasting relationships in my life. Allowing people to see the real you, flaws and all, is a gift, not a burden, and will only benefit you and them in the long run.

I'd also like you to remember that it's always okay to ask for help or guidance when you need it. This helps you to grow as a person, and it's how we all learn and develop into the best version of ourselves—by gaining the knowledge and insight that we need to thrive. The flip side of this is knowing and asserting your worth! Are you an expert in a given subject? Are you super-skilled at a particular job, hobby, or craft? Share that knowledge and experience with pride, making yourself the same foundation and fountain of wisdom that you can enjoy and expect from others in other areas. This is how we all work together to reach self-actualization and harmony.

If this all sounds a bit theoretical, don't worry: I've created a list of concrete ways you can find your inner assertiveness and manifest it to the outside world. Assertiveness has been called "the golden mean between passivity and aggression," which I think is a wonderful way of putting it: it is the sweet spot between letting people trample all over you and become cruel and domineering yourself as a reaction, neither of which are desirable, either in the context of your relationships, or for your own inner peace.

1. Set (and Maintain) Boundaries

While it might seem strange to set rules for yourself or your relationships, there is nothing damaging about boundaries: quite the opposite, actually. By setting and maintaining boundaries like "your mother is welcome to visit us on Saturday afternoons, not in the week," and "I can't drive you to that concert, but I can give you the code for a good rideshare app," and "my scheduled hours are 9 am to 6 pm, so I can't stay beyond six," you assert the worth of your time and resources to yourself and to others.

2. Be Active in Your Problem-Solving: Take Accountability

Unfortunately, it's rare that somebody swoops in and saves us from our problems in this world. But there is power and autonomy in taking your problems firmly by the reins and directing the course of your future. Once you realize that you are your own navigator and captain in this world, it can be a frightening and liberating thing, and it means taking on the good and the bad. If there is a problem in your life that needs solving, take it by the horns today, and bask in the relief and sudden freedom from anxiety when you realize it probably wasn't even as bad as you imagined.

3. Remember That Others Aren't Psychic

This tip is almost the emotional equivalent of the logistical advice above: when it comes to interpersonal conflicts or communications, remember that other people can't read your mind. If there is something troubling you, be sure to communicate it honestly and give them a chance to rectify whatever is bothering you. You might be surprised at the positive results! At the same time…

4. Other People's Feelings Are Not Your Responsibility

Of course, on this earth, we all have an obligation to be kind and considerate whenever we can. But you are not responsible for the actions, thoughts, or feelings of another person—you can only control your own, and even that can be a tricky skill to master!

Finally…

5. Give it Time…

Your newfound confidence and assertiveness may not manifest overnight, and you will almost certainly face challenges and setbacks along the way. This is normal and to be expected.

In the next section, we'll look at shyness and social phobia.

SHYNESS AND SOCIAL PHOBIA

What are these phenomena, and is there a difference between them? While it goes without saying that mental health is a complex matter with plenty of blurred lines and difficult to define categories and boundaries, generally speaking, shyness is a personality trait, and a social phobia is a mental condition that can cause the sufferer severe distress in social situations. The difference between these two is that, while a shy person may not enjoy being in the middle of a crowd or thrust into the spotlight, they will not feel the same agonizing, excruciating sensation of a person with a social phobia who's been thrown into the same situations. The same might apply to things like starting a new job, attending a party where one only knows the host, or even people singing happy birthday to you at a busy restaurant.

For shy people, this is unnerving. For people with a social phobia, it's unbearably painful.

Whether you're a shy person, or have a social phobia, and would like to be more confident and socially active, you can use the tips and tricks listed throughout these books and continue with your daily positive affirmations—by now, you must be an expert at them! And don't worry, there'll be plenty more at the end of this chapter to pad out your repertoire—be sure to read on to get to them soon!

But first, here is a legitimate and comprehensive, succinct guide to help you deal with shyness and social phobias:

WHAT CAUSES SHYNESS AND SOCIAL PHOBIAS?

In order to address shyness and social phobias, first, it will be helpful to look at their root cause. As we've touched upon in Chapters One to Four of this book, a lack of confidence, low self-esteem, shyness, and social phobias can all be caused or impacted by a wide variety of factors, all of which can be split into three main categories: social reasons, biological reasons, and psychological reasons.

Social Reasons: Anybody who's experienced bullying, abuse, neglect, manipulation, control, or continued negativity from others in their life is likely to be vulnerable to low self-confidence, low self-esteem, shyness, and social phobias. When we are told that we are in some way faulty, or that we don't matter, or that we are a burden, we internalize this messaging, and it degrades our sense of dignity and self-worth.

Biological Reasons: Did you know that you can have a biological predisposition to conditions like hormonal imbalances, chemical imbalances, depression, anxiety, and even conditions like substance abuse, bipolar disorder, borderline personality disorder, and PTSD? These conditions can be passed down through generations, especially considering that sometimes (but not always) people suffering from these disorders can inflict pain upon others (like their children), usually in situations where they have not been diagnosed or are unwilling or unable to access the help they need. Imagine a situation like the following: a father with a genetic predisposition towards depression doesn't realize that he's suffering from the condition; because of this, he treats his son in imperfect or harmful ways; his son, who's already inherited his father's predisposition towards depressive tendencies, becomes even more depressed than he might have been in another environment, because of his father's treatment of him. The biological and social reasons combine in a perfect storm, which is why it can sometimes be so difficult to unpick and untangle the source of our pain and misery to address and overcome it.

[Please note that in this scenario, I'm not blaming the hypothetical father for suffering from a medical condition he cannot control: I'm using the anecdote to demonstrate how slippery a concept of mental health can be and how it can go undetected amongst our loved ones —and even ourselves. I'm a prideful person, and it took me longer than I'm willing to admit before I finally threw up my hands and found the courage to acknowledge, to myself and my loved ones, that I was suffering from depression and anxiety. I felt ashamed, as if I could somehow overcome these things by the strength of will, and would have done so by now if I was strong enough. That idea is completely false, but it's a myth about mental health that I'd internalized.]

Psychological Reasons: Somewhere in the middle of the previous two sits the "psychological reasons" category. This relates to the spiralling, negative thoughts I mentioned while discussing the relative pros and cons of Cognitive Behavioural Therapy, CBT. If through biological or societal causes, we grow up to have low self-confidence, low self-esteem, social phobias, or a shy personality, we often end up reinforcing our negative beliefs about ourselves through our thought patterns.

For example, when we are feeling lonely, we might tell ourselves that it's because we have no friends, nobody likes us, and we are fundamentally unlikeable. When we are feeling unattractive, we might tell ourselves that we are objectively 'ugly'—when in reality, there is no such thing, and every person is beautiful in their own unique and irreplicable way. When we feel we don't have worth as a hobbyist or an employee, we might look at others we believe to be excelling and exceeding us and conclude that their success is due to their inherent 'superiority.' As you might have noticed, many of these thoughts can be rewired to reflect a more accurate version of reality. When we are lonely, it is rarely the case that we have no friends, or nobody likes us: when you are feeling this way, take a moment to remember that other people are probably wrapped up in the day to day stresses and insecurities of their own lives, and the fact that you haven't had a message, or they had to cancel plans the other day, is no reflection on their true feelings for you.

For example, a new father might have been too exhausted from caring for a newborn to meet you for that drink. Your high-powered CEO friend might be having a tough time at work and be unable to answer your calls, but that doesn't mean she isn't thinking of you and making a mental note to herself that she should reach out as soon as possible.

Simply put: we have no access to the inner workings of another person's mind, and when you have the choice to either assume the worst about them (and yourself) or the best, why not try assuming the best? Of course, there will always be a plethora of bad actors in the world—people who are selfish, inconsiderate, manipulative, and cruel—but their presence and existence shouldn't dim the brilliance of the kind and genuine people you've come to know and love, nor should the behaviour of a few bad people make you treat the ones you value with suspicion.

If you have a friend or loved one whose company you're missing, I'd like to set you a little challenge: set your ego aside for a moment (and I say this without judgment, as a person who has found it very difficult to overcome my hurt feelings in the past!), and reach out to them with sincerity and curiosity. Ask them how their life is going, and allow yourself to be vulnerable enough to say you miss them and would like to spend some time with them (either online or in person). You'll be amazed how open people can be to reconnecting—especially in our fast-paced modern world, where it's so easy to drop the ball and take each other for granted! I've been guilty of being on both sides of this situation.

For example, just today, a friend—with whom I lost touch for almost three years—messaged me to say that a book she'd read reminded her of me. She asked me if I still lived locally, and if I'd like to meet up and reconnect. The silly thing is, I'd been meaning to message her and say almost exactly the same thing, but so much time had passed that I felt embarrassed to do so! I thought she wouldn't welcome hearing from me. Her message was a lesson in both humility and my own self-worth: I had to remind myself that 1) I had acted poorly in neglecting her, but also, 2) people did care about me and want to be my friend, even almost three years after losing touch!

This is just one example of a negative thought that can be rewired and redirected before it negatively impacts our self-esteem. "Nobody likes me" becomes "my friends have been busy, but the good news is that I'm as capable of reaching out as they are, and they'll most likely be delighted to hear from me!" The same process can be applied to thoughts like "I'm ugly," or "I'm a bad employee/daughter/mother/girlfriend/wife"—dig a little deeper and interrogate the thought. Turn it around. Experiment in the safety of your own mind.

WHAT PERPETUATES THESE PATTERNS?

There are habits we can fall into that reinforce our social phobias, insecurities, and anxieties, and which can hurt our self-confidence and self-esteem. Three of these patterns are avoidance, safety behaviours, and increased self-focus. But what do these terms mean in the context of mental health and shyness?

Avoidance: This is pretty much what it sounds like. When we suffer from debilitating social anxiety or social phobias, it can be far easier to avoid going out in public or facing social situations altogether. This might look like cancelling party plans, declining to accept an award, wanting a relationship but not putting yourself out there and going on dates, staying home to watch a movie instead of joining your friends at a museum or bar, or even, in severe situations, turning off or ignoring your phone, because even digital interactions are too much for you to deal with at that particular moment in time.

Now, none of these behaviours is by definition bad things—we all want a Netflix night now and then! It's not unhealthy to enjoy your own company and stay home to work on your hobbies or have a relaxing evening away from your usual obligations. Avoidance becomes a problem when it's motivated by fear rather than desire—or, to put it differently, when we avoid social situations in which we actually want to participate.

Have you ever got all dolled up in your best outfit, hair, and make-up (if make-up's your thing) only to cancel at the very last second, despite being excited to go out? Have you ever turned down a date you'd have been excited for because you felt too painfully shy? Have you ever worked hard on a project or endeavour, only to back away from accepting the award that is yours because the thought of standing on a stage and receiving the praise you deserve made you want to curl up in a ball and cry? That's the point at which avoidance has become a coping mechanism and not a once-in-a-while retreat from the busy world around you.

Safety Behaviours: Okay. So, say you wanted to practice avoidance, but you've been forced to attend a social event—like, say, an important family wedding—that you couldn't beg out of. This is where safety behaviours can come into play. Does any of the following sound like you?

- Remaining quiet or even silent during conversations

- Avoiding eye contact with people around you
- Following around the one person you know—or hanging out with the pets!
- Relying excessively on substances like drugs or alcohol to overcome your inhibitions

If so, you might be practising safety behaviours. If there is a habit or mental crutch that you rely upon to 'get through' social events (like being in control of your own ride, or staying with the host, or dressing demurely so as not to 'stand out'), you might be suffering from social anxiety or phobias, or might just be a shy person. Again, it's a matter of degree: if these safety behaviours inhibit your enjoyment of the activity, or if you feel you need them to 'survive' an outing, that speaks to a fairly severe case of low self-confidence and low self-esteem that might benefit from some CBT and positive affirmations.

Increased Self-Awareness: This safety behaviour can be a horrible snake eating its own tail. What I mean by this is that increased self-awareness, which kicks in when we are already feeling anxious, can make us feel more anxious, and in doing so, perpetuates itself and our own social discomfort. If you feel that the (literal or metaphorical) spotlight has been turned on you in an event or conversation, you might become aware that your knees are shaking, your heart is racing, your palms are sweaty, your throat is dry, or you have a sinking sensation in your stomach. This, in turn, convinces you that everybody else can see your anxiety and gives you the impression that you are not 'performing well' socially, which only impedes your confidence, self-image, and self-esteem further.

You might become so hyper-aware of your physical state (or your racing thoughts) that you stammer over your words, turn pale, or blush, thus becoming visibly anxious and unintentionally giving off signals that you're not having a good time, which can make socializing, especially with new people, difficult. And I know what you're thinking—this is hardly fair! It's horrible to feel 'punished' for anxiety, especially when we put ourselves out there and genuinely do try to make connections. Unfortunately, I'm just describing a phenomenon that some, if not all of us, experience.

RECOGNIZING PATTERNS OF UNHELPFUL THINKING

In the previous section, we covered how and why conditions like social anxiety and phobias can manifest, which is the first step to dealing with them. I also began to illustrate some of the patterns of unhelpful thinking we can fall into: here, I'm going to give them explicit names so that you can label them and pluck them from the garden of your mind like the life-choking weeds they are.

Mind Reading: This is when we convince ourselves that we know what another person is thinking. "They thought I was a total dork," "He would never be attracted to me," "She's already decided not to give me the promotion because she hates my work." As I mentioned earlier, remember that we have no idea what's going on in other people's heads! Don't create stress and anxiety for yourself by trying to pre-empt their thoughts and opinions—that way lies misery.

Labelling: This one is pretty simple. We give ourselves reductive labels like 'lazy,' 'boring,' 'shy,' 'unlikable.' Ask yourself: is there any other person in your life, even one, even your most distant acquaintance, to whom you'd ascribe one single word as the sum of their entire lived experience and personality? No? I thought not. I bet you think of them as "Betty from accounting, who likes motorbiking, has four cats, and is always late replying to emails," or "Paul, who doesn't drink, adopted a son from Thailand last year, and once called me by the wrong name," or "Sam, who sells homemade lavender soap on Etsy and who once dented my car and didn't apologize."

Notice how these impressions combine the good, the bad, and the neutral, which is how 99.9% of people will perceive you! Grant yourself the same nuance and understanding of the whole that you grant to others. Nobody is 'just' a daughter, mother, lover, friend, employee, or partner. How 'good' or 'bad' you are at these roles (which is itself a reductive label!) is irrelevant to the worth of the whole. Stop chopping yourself up into little fragments! You are a fully realized and complicated human being with flaws and strengths. The labels you apply to yourself could never encompass or describe the reality, so ditch them.

Predicting the Future: This could otherwise be described as a defeatist attitude. When you go into a situation with the preconceived idea that you will fail or be poorly received, you can often create a self-fulfilling prophecy. If you were interviewing candidates for a job, who would you rather hire: the person who has entered the interview, already certain that they're not good enough, and constantly derides and downplays their skills, talents, and experience? Or the person who calmly and confidently answers your questions and tells you exactly how and why she's the right woman for the job? The first candidate had 'predicted the future' by assuring herself that she would fail: her attitude then made this a reality. The second candidate did the opposite: she manifested the result she wanted through confidence and positive thinking (even if she secretly felt shy, lacking in confidence the entire time!)

Overgeneralizing: Overgeneralising is when we take an isolated incident and mentally convert it into a pattern or inaccurate universal 'truth.' This might sound like, "I always fail interviews," "I never get a date," or "everybody thinks I'm no fun to be around," or "my whole family hates me." Notice how the language doesn't leave any space for compromise or contradiction? A more accurate interpretation of these thoughts, respectively, might be, "I failed at this interview," or "I was rejected for this date," or "one person said I was no fun," or "I had an argument with my sister about a specific issue."

Do you see how I rewrote these thoughts to make them specific to the incident that caused them and took away their power as universal 'truths'? By digging into the specifics of an emotion or perception and not letting yourself blow it up into an analysis of your situation or relationship as a whole, you avoid damaging your self-esteem.

Focusing Only on the Negative: we've all done this at some point. After an event, have you gone home cringing about the drink you spilt or the faux pas you made? I bet you've mentally lingered on small social mistakes like these and forgotten or neglected to think back on the pleasant moments! When you focus solely on what you did "wrong," you do yourself a disservice: at other times throughout the night, I promise people will have found you beautiful, witty, charming, polite, and kind—it's important to allow these perceptions, too, into your mind, to counteract and balance out the negative of your mistakes (which everybody makes, and which only you are likely to remember anyway).

WAYS TO CHALLENGE AN UNHELPFUL THOUGHT

If you suspect you might be mind-reading, labelling, predicting the future, overgeneralizing, or focusing only on the negative, and you're either not sure you're doing so, or would like to address the fact that you are, the good news is that I've compiled a series of questions (below) to help you out.

1. Can I provide or think of any evidence against this thought?

For example, if you think a presentation at work went poorly, can you identify any positive reactions in the form of nods, smiles, verbal praise, or general agreement with your ideas? What about encouraging questions asking you to elucidate?

2. Can I provide or think of any evidence for this thought?

If you believe that your partner's family hates you, do you have specific proof of this? Have they told you, to your face, that you are unwanted or unwelcome? Has your partner told you they've communicated a dislike of you? My guess is, the answer's "no," right?

Lots of insecurities can't hold up when interrogated and bared to the harsh light of day.

3. Can I notice any patterns of unhelpful thinking from the last section?

Do you suspect you could be mind-reading, labelling, predicting the future, overgeneralizing, or focusing only on the negative?

4. What would I say to a friend if they were dealing with this?

My guess is that you'd support them, offer comfort, and reassure them that their negative views about themselves were inaccurate, right? If your friend was anxious about attending a party, you'd probably say something like, "You're a kind, fun person, who always brings something valuable to the conversation, and you look amazing. It's not your job to make sure the whole night goes perfectly, everyone has a good time, and other people will be too focused on their own business or insecurities to judge you. They'll be happy to meet you!" Offer the same grace to yourself.

5. Could I look at this situation in another way?

Instead of thinking, "I'm a stupid baby for worrying about this exam", why not rewire that thought to something along the lines of, "It's normal and okay to worry about an exam that will impact my future, but no matter how it goes, I will be okay, and this result will not affect my worth as a person or a woman."

6. Is there a proactive solution I can find to this unhelpful thought?

There is immense freedom in finding the courage to ask for help and validation! If you're nervous about a social event, ask the host or a guest you already know who they think you'll get along with. If you're feeling insecure about faux pas, ask your friend if they think anybody cared or even noticed! You'll be surprised how useful these little lifelines from others can be in navigating stormy social waters.

ADDITIONAL ACTIVITY: USE AND ABUSE THE POINTS SYSTEM!

If you struggle to put yourself out there, one method that some women have found useful is to create a points system to reward themselves for doing things that frighten them or take them out of their comfort zone. For example, small talk with the shopkeeper might be worth 2 points, going to a party might be worth 5, and giving a speech to a crowd might be 10. Create as many categories as you need. Create milestones for certain amounts, like 25, 50, or 100 points, and reward yourself accordingly.

Five points might be worth a new book that you've had your eye on and been meaning to read for a while, or a nice glass of wine. 25 points might be a nice takeaway meal. 100 points might be an afternoon at a luxury spa.

If you're the artsy type, you might enjoy indulging your creativity and whipping up a beautiful chart or page in your notebook to keep track of this. Alternatively, if you're more mathematically or technologically-minded (not that a person can't be both!), you might enjoy setting up a spreadsheet or an automated system on your phone. Have fun with it! This is a form of exposure therapy that will give you an incentive to actively push your boundaries and explore.

Best of luck!

In the next chapter, we'll build on what we've covered here by taking a deep dive into compassion and being kind to yourself.

AFFIRMATIONS

- I am strong, powerful, and fearless.
- My fears do not define me.
- My fears do not own me.
- My fears do not control me.
- My fears have kept me safe from harm in the past.
- My fears are not wrong or evil; I simply need to make a choice about whether or not they serve me.
- I trust my instincts, but I challenge my thought processes.
- I keep my mind active and questioning.
- I am endlessly curious about myself, and the way I want others to be.
- I grant myself the same grace and understanding I give to others.
- My self-doubts are not necessarily accurate.
- My negative thoughts are not necessarily accurate.

- My friends and loved ones DO want to spend time with me.
- I DO provide interesting conversation.
- I AM fun to be around.
- I AM a good employee, but that is not all I am.
- I AM a good partner, but that is not all I am.
- I AM a good girlfriend, but that is not all I am.
- I AM a good wife, but that is not all I am.
- I AM a good parent, but that is not all I am.
- I AM a good daughter, but that is not all I am.
- I AM a good aunt, but that is not all I am.
- I AM a good niece, but that is not all I am.
- I AM a good grandmother, but that is not all I am.
- I am not defined by my family roles.
- I am not defined by my professional roles.
- I am not defined by whether or not I am in a romantic relationship.
- I cultivate and nourish the relationships I have.
- I seek new connections while honouring the old.
- I deserve to take up space.
- I am enough as I am.
- I interrogate myself to work towards continuous growth.
- I thrive.

EXERCISE

Find four ways to "raise your voice" this week. This could mean:

- Correcting somebody when they insult you or make a false assumption about you. *"I'm not 'the girl at reception,' I am a valued administrator with multiple degrees and years of experience. I am a woman and a professional, not a child."*
- Speaking up when a marginalized friend, co-worker, or stranger is subjected to bigotry. *"That is racist/classist/sexist/ableist/homophobic/transphobic/fatphobic. If you continue to talk to my friend or me that way, I will leave the conversation."*
- Making your needs heard by your family, friends, or partner. *"I would appreciate it if you could listen to me and validate my feelings when I'm upset, instead of just telling me everything will be okay. You're probably right, but when you say that at the moment, it feels dismissive of my emotional state."*
- Setting clear boundaries and sticking to them. *"I'm sorry, but as I mentioned on Monday, I can't work this Friday. But good luck finding somebody else to cover the shift."*

6
FACE YOUR FEARS

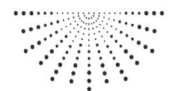

In the last chapter, we looked at the topic of social shyness and social phobias and anxieties. These topics go hand in hand with the fear of social rejection. What is social rejection, and why do we feel it so sorely? How can we respond positively to criticism in a way that benefits our learning and our growth? Similarly, what is fear of failure, and can it ever be a good thing? How can we handle mistakes and forgive ourselves in order to move on once we've messed up socially or at work?

This chapter will provide the answers to these questions and more, and of course, at the back of the chapter, you'll find affirmations written specifically to help you face your fears, overcome the fear of social rejection and criticism, and let go of the past, and any small errors you might have made.

WHY DO WE FEAR?

Before looking at how we can conquer our fears, it will be helpful to know why we experience fear in the first place. Fear is an evolutionary instinct that served us particularly well when we were early humans: life was fraught with predators, hostile environments, and other dangers, and those who didn't learn to listen to their gut and develop an unerring sense of when their safety was at risk didn't last very long in that brutal prehistoric world.

The thing is, our brains are very resistant to change, which is why, years later, they're still programmed to react to, say, a hostile email, in the same way, we would typically respond to a sabre-toothed tiger attempting to eat us: utter, abject, stomach-clenching, mouth-drying terror. This isn't because you're overdramatic or too sensitive: biologically, we're designed to seek out and recognize what we perceive as threats to our safety, and these days, an annoyed partner or boss, or a social rejection, come under that category.

You might have heard this described as the "fight or flight" response, but there are actually five common instinctive responses to fear-inducing stimuli. These are:

- The "Fight Response"
- The "Flight Response"
- The "Freeze Response"
- The "Fawn Response"
- The "Flop Response"

I will now go over what each of these means.

Fight: The fight response, in addition to the flight response, is one of the two most well-known responses to fear-inducing stimuli. Our adrenaline kicks in, our muscles tense and ready themselves for battle, and our hearts begin to race, preemptively oxygenating our bodies and brains for the fight it believes is coming. This is why some people, when frightened—at 'haunted house' events or when they are startled—will unthinkingly lash out at the cause. I've heard of scare actors being punched, kicked, or shoved, not deliberately, but out of pure instinct by members of the public. Even though the guests at these attractions *know logically* that the threat is contrived for entertainment reasons, the older part of their brain, the reptile part, kicks in and lashes out. Fight response.

Flight: The opposite of the fight response is the flight response, meaning 'to take flight,' or in other words, to flee. People with the flight response will physically run, cringe, crawl or hide away from the threat—anything to avoid directly confronting it. This doesn't mean that they are cowards! There are many situations in which humans understand they're outmatched, and their chances of survival will be better if they don't confront or antagonize that which is threatening them. People with a flight response feel a strong and undeniable need to get *away from the threat* by any means possible.

Freeze: This is what it sounds like. Sometimes, in response to a threat, we simply freeze up. I have an intense phobia of worms, and my response to them, when I find one on the ground, is somewhere between the "flight" and "freeze:" I feel a deep and instinctive sense of revulsion and disgust to the point that I feel nauseous, and shivers course up and down my body. I want to get as far away from the worm as I physically can—that would be a flight response.

However, at the same time, I also feel a need to keep my eyes directly on the "threat" the worm presents, and I often find myself unable to do anything except stare obsessively at the worm, frozen and unsure what to do. This is a classic example of the freeze response: an extended, endless moment of agonizing indecision. Sometimes, doing nothing, and taking no assertive action, can feel like the "safest" option, as we give ourselves time to strategize and gather our mental and physical resources. Again, though, I'd like to reiterate that none of this happens *consciously*: our fight, flight, freeze, fawn, or flop responses are decided on instinctively, instantaneously, and they can vary, even within one person, from event to event (or threat to threat).

Fawn: To fawn is to attempt to win the favour of, distract, or submit to the perpetrator. Sadly, this is a response that many victims of abuse develop at a young age (though they can also develop and rely upon any of the other responses, too). We attempt to disarm the threat by either appeasing it, showing it that we, in turn, are not a threat, or showing it that we are not 'worth' its trouble.

In the animal kingdom, you see this all the time. A dog submits to a power struggle with another. Cats, to express trust, will blink slowly to demonstrate that they feel comfortable closing their eyes around you and therefore don't perceive you as a threat. Humans do the same in many overt and subtle ways. This can be as obvious as showing one's palms, backing off, and verbally expressing that you don't want any trouble, or it can be as subtle as looking down and to the side or adjusting your body language to make yourself smaller. Even in situations where the conflict is more insidious and unspoken than physical, many victims of bullying or abuse will attempt to laugh off a perpetrator's threatening advances by pretending that it's a joke they're already in on or downplay the conflict by defending the perpetrator: "Oh, I know he doesn't mean it, it's okay, we're not fighting—no, I don't need help, thank you."

At this point, I'd like to point out that none of these responses is a choice, and none is braver, better, or more appropriate than any other—they're just atavistic instincts we carry and embody after millennia of evolution.

Flop: Finally, we have the flop response. Sometimes, when a threat seems unbearable or insurmountable, human beings simply... tap out. By which I mean our nervous systems shut everything down, and we lose consciousness. A subtler form of this could be feeling dizzy, seeing spots, feeling as if time is moving differently, or suddenly feeling unimaginably exhausted—more so than you have ever felt.

All of us know what it's like to face a threat that triggers these responses, no matter which one (or several you embody). I'd like, at this point, to include a quick word about PTSD (Post Traumatic Stress Disorder) and CPTSD (Complicated Post Traumatic Stress Disorder). Often caused by events or periods of immense distress, these conditions leave the sufferer in a near-constant state of one of these responses. Their brain is always flooded with cortisol, the reactionary stress hormone, and their brain literally feels and reacts as if it is constantly under siege from the threat of their past, which the person then projects onto current, perceived threats. If this sounds like you—if you live in a constant state of fear, and one of the fight, flight, freeze, fawn, or flop responses—you may benefit from and be entitled to help beyond that which this book can provide. Of course, this book provides techniques that are helpful for everyone, but it's fine to use multiple tools in conjunction with one another. Attack the problem from all angles!

FEAR OF REJECTION

Having introduced the topic of fear and how it can present itself in different personalities, let's look at a specific fear, one universally acknowledged and grimaced at: the fear of rejection.

Social bonds are extremely important to humans: we suffer without them, and they're what kept us alive in our early days. They're what keep us alive today: think of the motherly instinct to nurture her child or the fatherly instinct to protect his family (though people of all genders feel both of these impulses, I'm just using the expressions as shorthand). Therefore, fear of rejection—like fear itself!—once served a healthy, evolutionary purpose. Rejection can also strengthen our resilience and force us to dig deep for mental resources and fortitude we didn't even know we had! But it's no good when it gets in the way of our happiness, our social lives, or our personal and professional development. With that in mind, here are some tips for using the pain of rejection to your advantage:

Learn From It: Everybody, at one point in their life, gets rejected, whether the rejection is personal, professional, romantic, or utterly random. When this happens, ask yourself: what have I learned from this? What skills have I gathered? What have I realized about myself? What did I observe about the person or party rejecting me? If this is something I want, what can I do better next time?

Remember when we talked about growth mindsets? Learning from rejection is something that a person with a growth mindset does.

Investigate Critical Thoughts: When you're having critical thoughts about yourself, probe and investigate them, the way I taught you to in the previous chapter. Are they inaccurate, or are you falling into unhelpful patterns, like mind reading or overgeneralizing? It can be very easy to do so after a rejection, which makes us feel very vulnerable, so keep an eye out! Your brain will try to blame you for the rejection, to find a reason that *you* deserved it—don't let it do so.

Build Yourself Up: To counteract the negative thoughts that might crop up, after a rejection, indulge in some deliberate and targeted positivity! Indulge isn't quite the right word, because positivity shouldn't be a rare luxury, doled out only as a reward, or on special occasions: positivity should be a muscle we exercise and put through conditioning drills every day!

If you're feeling sad following a rejection, use the positive affirmations in this book, write down five positive facts about yourself, or ask for compliments from your friends, family, or loved ones. You could even wear that special outfit that makes you feel like a million dollars, or spray a bit of your favourite perfume on your wrists so that its scent can help you feel glamorous and calm. These little rituals aren't a substitute for long-term solutions or medical help, but what they can do is give you the strength to get through the *current moment*. And sometimes—no, *always*—that's enough.

Reach Out: After a rejection, we can feel lonely and unwanted. To counteract this, spend some time nourishing and developing the relationships you do have. Go out for a drink with friends, or a walk. Have a crafting day or a movie night together. Work out together at the gym. Bake a pie in their familiar kitchen while you catch up over coffee. Whatever it takes to make you feel connected and safe.

Reaching out can also look like joining a dating website, sending an email to an old teacher or colleague you appreciate, or getting your parents a random gift or bunch of flowers, "just because." Paradoxically, serving others socially makes us feel more valued and less alone. By expressing to somebody what they mean to you, you'll feel wanted and loved in return!

Keep Your Distance: This might seem like a contradiction—after all, it seems to directly go against the previous tip. What I'm advising is that you keep a little distance—if only temporarily—from the person or party that rejected you. While feelings are still stinging and the wound is still bleeding, no good can come of emailing that company and asking *why* they didn't want to hire you or calling that guy you went on a date to try and change his mind and get him to go out with you again. Nor should you spend your evenings searching through the social media pages of the people that hurt your feelings: nothing you find there will make you feel better, but you might find something that makes you feel a whole load of a lot worse. It's simply not worth it.

If you want to reconnect or reapply *after* you've had time to get over your hurt and work on yourself, that's okay, but let it scab first. There's no rush (though a desire for the nebulous concept of 'closure' can often convince us otherwise).

RESPONDING TO CRITICISM

Criticism, though it can feel like a form of rejection, is subtly different from a personal rejection, and in a professional or creative context, it can be useful. It can, however, also hurt our feelings and damage our self-confidence, self-image, and self-esteem, especially if we don't know how to handle it or how to respond to it properly. This section will teach you how to separate the good criticism from the bad and how to deal with each kind as it comes.

Good criticism is delivered kindly and calmly. It is specific to the issue at hand and doesn't attack you as a person. It is objective and coupled with suggestions for improvement.

Bad criticism is delivered with anger or malice. It attacks you as a person, blaming your inherent personality traits for the failure or problem and using the issue at hand as an example of how you are universally [insert bad trait here]. It is highly subjective and doesn't come with any suggestions for improvement (because the person delivering it isn't interested in your improvement; they're interested in your humiliation and misery and want to see you beaten down).

Examples of good criticism:

"Chapter two is strong, but in chapter three, I didn't understand the heroine's motivation: I'd suggest going back and making her reasons for her behaviour clearer to the reader."

"This was a wonderful tomato sauce, but I found it a bit acidic and salty for my taste. Next time, why don't you consider adding some sugar or honey to balance those flavours out?"

"You're getting a lot stronger in your upper body, but I'm not seeing as much improvement in your leg muscles: why don't we schedule more days for leg training?"

Notice how these examples include a (sincere) compliment, the criticism at hand, and a suggestion? They don't talk about the person's skills or commitment as a whole; rather, the criticism and feedback are offered as an opportunity for learning in a specific area.

Examples of bad criticism:

"You can't wear that; you look hideous."

"That presentation was a shambles. All of it was worthless."

"I can't eat this. It's disgusting."

"I can't believe how weak you are—are you even trying?"

These responses are demeaning, sarcastic, non-specific, unnecessarily personal, and unhelpful.

Remember the difference between good and bad criticism when you're asked for honest feedback.

So. How should you respond to each kind?

Well, when you receive bad criticism, like the examples listed above, congratulations—I hereby give you permission to completely ignore it! Anybody who would talk to you like this is not invested in your wellbeing, your development, or your improvement, and their opinion is not worth taking seriously.

Often people levy cruel criticism like this in order to drag others down and make themselves feel bigger and more important, but their insecurities are not your problem to solve, nor do you exist to be their punching bag. Whether it's out of jealousy, spite, insecurity, or simply a mean personality, they are not speaking from a kind and truthful place. Bless their heart, with maybe a sad smile for the angry torment they're trapped in, and move on.

When you receive good criticism, do your best to respond with grace and positivity. And, listen, I do get it: even good criticism delivered kindly and with the best interests at heart can sting—even when it comes from a loved one! I'd urge you to remember that somebody who has taken the time to honestly, thoughtfully, evaluate your work —and who is being vulnerable and risking their relationship with you in the process!—deserves the courtesy of being heard, acknowledged, and thanked for their feedback, even if, upon further consideration, you privately decide that you disagree. That's totally okay! Take what positives you can from that experience.

When receiving either good or bad criticism, it's important, for your dignity and peace of mind, not to respond in anger. By lashing out in vengeance at somebody who has delivered bad criticism, you are sinking to their level, and you lose the moral high ground. And friends who have given you good criticism don't deserve to be snapped at or threatened just because you're feeling insecure. Remain the bigger woman, always.

That is *not* to say that you should accept abuse without protest: there are ways to assert yourself and your boundaries without endangering, embarrassing, or lowering yourself and the high standards you deserve.

FEAR OF FAILURE

How many of us have had the archetypal dream: we're late for a test, we haven't studied, and also—upon looking down, we realize—we're naked! This type of stress dream reflects a pretty universal anxiety and problem: fear of failure. It's something lots of us can relate to, but what does it mean, exactly?

Lived experiences—events in our past or criticisms from our loved ones—can leave us with a fear of what we consider to be 'failure.' You might define failure as ending a relationship or underperforming in a test, or being rejected for a job (all of which, by the way, can be blessings in disguise), to name just a few. Here is how a fear of failure can manifest itself:

Hesitation: You might demonstrate a reluctance to get involved in projects and initiatives, even if the cause or outcome is something about which you're deeply passionate! Have you put off volunteering at your local soup kitchen, or auditioning for that play, or starting your own business? If so, a fear of failure may be holding you back.

Self-sabotage: Have you ever deliberately procrastinated on a project, or not handed in an important piece of work, or ghosted somebody you care about, just so that you could say to yourself afterwards that your 'failure' was of your own choosing? Sometimes, the only way we feel we can regain control of a situation is to blow it up ourselves before anybody else can.

This can also manifest in subtler ways: have you ever put yourself down in conversation or made self-deprecating jokes? This could be an example of fear of social 'failure:' you might have thoughts along the lines of, "everybody *already thinks* I'm boring or ugly, so if I make a joke about it, I'll at least be showing that I'm not oblivious to the fact—I'm in on the joke, and I know I'm unattractive or undesirable to be around." If you've done this before (I know I have), you may not be aware that it's actually a form of self-sabotage. You're harpooning yourself socially instead of giving yourself a real chance to succeed and shine.

Perfectionism: This is a demon that many of us have on our shoulders. I have lost count of the times I've put something off until I could do it "better" (and, considering "better" is a relative term, this meant never doing the thing at all). I recently took up sewing, and though I felt confident enough making cushions and bunting, I put off graduating to making garments because I knew I would make mistakes. If I couldn't produce a perfect dress or skirt, I didn't want to bother. I didn't want to expend that effort and energy on a result that I would find embarrassing. But this is exactly how we learn, especially when taking up a new skill! It's not humiliating to stumble and grow through trial and error—it's admirable. After all, do you want to stagnate as a person, never expanding your horizons or skill sets, or do you want to fall, graze your knees, survive, and get back up again a better-informed and stronger person?

HOW TO COPE WITH FEAR OF FAILURE

1. Reframe it: To begin with, I would suggest challenging the concept of 'failure' altogether. The Western world especially places an unhealthy emphasis on black and white thinking: we either succeeded in a test, or we failed. We got the job, or we didn't. We got married, or we broke up.

But actually, the space for learning, growth, and development between those two absolutes is an immense and nuanced spectrum. You might only get 2/10 on a test, for example, but you would come away from that test knowing the areas in which you needed to strengthen your knowledge. You may be unsuccessful in applying for a job, but you gained valuable CV-writing and interviewing experience and learned a little more about your chosen industry. Plus, you probably put yourself on the company's radar for any positions that open up in the future (provided you acted positively!).

And a relationship ending can sometimes be a far healthier and happier result than two people continuing to stay together for the wrong reasons. When something ends or doesn't go as planned, instead of mentally framing it as a 'failure,' try to think about what you've learned from the experience and what new doors, avenues, and options it's opened up for you. There is always a positive perspective that can be reached if you do a little soul-searching.

2. Analyze all the possible outcomes: This is a form of mental exposure therapy. By mentally rehearsing the 'failure' before it happens and planning for it, you can take the sting out of it if it does happen. But by also planning for the best outcome at the same time, you prepare yourself to succeed and put yourself in a winner's mindset. It's a cliché for a reason: prepare for the worst, hope for the best.

3. Set small goals (to fail!): As I mentioned when discussing the fear of rejection, it's possible to combat fear by setting and achieving small goals. Allow yourself to fail! I'm not suggesting you deliberately flunk out of school or drop all your important clients at work, but if you happen to miss an appointment or a deadline or underperform in an area where you'd like to improve, sit with that feeling a while, and realize that the world hasn't ended.

Apologize and move on. Forgive yourself as easily as others will forgive you. It's okay. Nobody else in this world is perfect, so you have no obligation to be either.

HANDLING YOUR MISTAKES (AND HOW TO MOVE ON)

If, however, the above bullet points still leave you cringing and anxious at the thought of failure or rejection, this section is designed to help you handle your mistakes and move on from mess-ups and faux pas.

1. Acknowledge Your Feelings: Name and acknowledge your feelings without giving them power over you. In meditative practice, one common exercise is to visualize the inner workings of your mind as if they are a river: watch your thoughts drift by in the current without jumping in and letting them sweep you away. Say to yourself, without emotion or judgment, "I am feeling scared of failure," or "I feel rejected," or "I'm embarrassed because I messed up." Then…

2. Rewrite Your Thoughts: Rewrite your thoughts to be more positive and affirming. Instead of thinking, "I failed because I'm unqualified," rewrite that thought to be, "I am qualified, but there were lots of qualified candidates: the fact that I didn't succeed this time isn't a reflection on me."

3. Try To See The Funny Side (Or Keep Perspective): At the end of the day, no humiliation or perceived failure, no matter how devastating it seemed at the time, is as awful as it seems, and the agony has diminishing returns. There are things I said and did as a teenager that felt like the end of the world at the time: now I can wince and shake my head at just how much I had to learn. Remind yourself, also, that you never have any idea what the future holds: what seems like the end of an opportunity today might have pushed you towards a far superior path, one you'd never even imagined would be open to you. Keep the event in perspective, and try to see the funny side. I promise it won't always hurt!

4. Apologize (Briefly) and Offer a Solution: If you messed up, apologize, briefly (but don't overdo it, and don't verbally castigate yourself or go off on a monologue about what a terrible person you are—this only makes the whole situation more difficult for everybody), and then *offer a solution*. Your communication might go something like this: "Hi Jim, I'm sorry that I missed yesterday's deadline for the teapot project: I have already contacted the client and plan to have the final draft finished by the end of business today." That's all you need to say! Most people are so busy with their own projects and problems that they rarely notice other people's mistakes, but even if they do, this is all you need to do to correct them. They'll soon forget it ever happened and move on. However…

5. Actions Count More than Words: If you've made a mistake, especially in a professional setting, your actions count more than your words. What do I mean by this? Well, if you send a message like the one above, apologizing and resolving to improve, and then simply… don't… the quality of your word and your promises has been undermined. You've demonstrated that your apologies are empty, and your resolutions to improve are insincere. So, always back up your word with definitive action, and regain trust in tangible ways. When you do this, you'll be amazed at how forgiving and understanding reasonable people can be.

AFFIRMATIONS

- I am allowed to make mistakes.
- How I handle my mistakes demonstrates my character.
- I acknowledge my feelings and let them drift past me.
- I back up my words with deeds.
- I move through the world, finding humour and positivity in everything.
- I confront my fears head-on.
- I take the sting out of a failure by forgiving my imperfections.
- A rejection is not a reflection on me.
- Failure is a chance to learn.
- Rejection is a chance to grow.
- I actively practise compassion and understanding.
- My fear responses are natural, evolutionary instincts: I am not wrong for feeling them.
- I have the power to reframe my thoughts, fears, and anxieties.
- Nobody is watching me as closely as I fear they are.
- People want me to succeed.
- My loved ones are cheering me on.

- I apologize sincerely for my mistakes and then forgive myself.
- Even flawed, I am worthy of love and respect.
- I give myself permission to mess up sometimes!
- I do not hesitate: I jump in headfirst.
- I am not a prisoner to my fears—I reach out and grasp my freedom.
- I will no longer be a slave to my perfectionist instincts.
- "Perfect" is the enemy of "done," but "done" is "perfect!"
- I will no longer self-sabotage. Instead, I will self-celebrate.

EXERCISE

Do three things that scare you this month—set yourself tasks!

For example:

- Challenge yourself to make small talk with five strangers this week.
- Apply for that job you've been too nervous to go for.
- Try a new hobby, and embrace the fact that you'll probably be less than amazing at it—to begin with!
- If you've been wanting to date but have procrastinated doing so out of anxiety, put yourself out there by joining a dating app, or asking a friend to set you up with someone.

7
SELF-COMPASSION AND SELF-LOVE

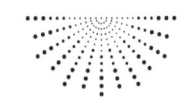

By now, you have a solid understanding of how and why we can end up with low self-confidence and low self-esteem, and I hope you've found the wisdom in this book to be relevant and useful so far. In this chapter, I'd like to explore the subject of self-love and self-compassion. We'll go over what exactly these concepts mean and how you can practice them.

WHAT ARE SELF-LOVE AND SELF-COMPASSION?

Self-love and self-compassion can be described as a state of knowing and accepting yourself for who you truly are, without criticism or judgment, and realizing that even on your worst days, you are worthy of love and respect. Self-love and self-compassion involve actively taking care of and advocating for yourself.

Sometimes, this means pushing yourself to reach your goals; at other times, it means listening to your body and allowing yourself to take a break. A person with self-love and self-compassion has a robust enough sense of self and worth that their self-esteem is not negatively impacted by a one-off event, like a rejection, a failure, a mistake they made, or criticism from others. But if you're still a little unsure about what these concepts might look like, here are some examples:

- A high-achieving student who fails a test but can say to herself, *"Not everybody can succeed 100% of the time, and I know that I tried my best: I am still a good student."*
- A stressed-out mother who raises her voice at her child in anger, who later says to herself, *"I am not a bad mother, I am just a flawed human being, like everybody else, who experienced a moment of weakness. I will apologize to my daughter, forgive myself, and move on while taking steps not to repeat my shouting episode in the future."*
- A woman who gossips about her husband to his work friends and later regrets it, but says to herself, *"I realize that what I did was wrong, and while I forgive myself, I will not do it again. Overall, I am a good wife who made a mistake."*

- A woman who doesn't get the promotion she was hoping for, but says to herself, *"I am still a good worker and a valued employee; this simply wasn't my time for an upward move."*

Self-love doesn't mean making excuses for our behaviours or refusing to hold ourselves accountable for harmful actions. Quite the opposite: it means acknowledging them head-on, doing what we can to rectify them, *and then moving on* without mentally punishing ourselves for all eternity.

"Okay," I hear you say, "If it's that easy, why doesn't everybody automatically have self-love and self-compassion?" That's a good question. The answer is this: much like low self-confidence and low self-esteem, a lack of self-love and self-compassion can be caused by lots of different biological, social, and psychological factors. Women are often socialized to prioritize the comfort, needs, ambitions, and happiness of others above themselves. We are taught that it's our place to make sure our partners, employers, families, and friends are fulfilled and secure while neglecting our own needs. So we end up putting ourselves last in the pecking order.

Over time, this can degrade our dignity and sense of self-worth. How often have you said some variation of, "I don't have time for a haircut, I have to take the kids to football practice?" or, "I can't go back to school while my husband is studying: one of us needs to earn an income." Or, "I can't go on holiday while my mother-in-law is sick: it's my job to take care of her." Self-love means realigning your priorities and realizing that you, too, matter. Not more than everybody else, but to at least the same extent.

WHY WE PUT OURSELVES LAST

There are many reasons we fall into the habit of putting ourselves last. For example:

We associate self-care with selfishness: We see any attempt to care for ourselves or prioritize our own happiness as taking away love, resources, and time from those who 'matter more': therefore, we think we're selfish for expending energy on ourselves rather than other people. It can be especially difficult to take time out when you're naturally a very giving person who gets joy out of helping others.

But consider this: 'carer burnout' is a very real thing. You *need* time to yourself and time spent on your own education, hobbies, interests, and inner peace in order to build up the resilience and strength you need to be of help to others! Have you ever heard the expression that you can't run on empty batteries? Well, that's what a person with little or no self-love and self-compassion is trying to do, and it takes a toll. Invest in yourself. It's the opposite of selfishness.

We feel a need to 'rescue' others: Have you ever attempted to 'fix' a cruel or ignorant romantic partner? A neglectful parent? An addict? Do you take the troubles of the world unto yourself and consider it your duty to remedy problems that aren't even related to you (like your friend's cousin who's been kicked out of her apartment and needs somewhere to stay, so you offer up your own sofa)? Have you stayed involved in a professional, romantic, or familial relationship because you saw the 'potential' in a person or a company to be better, despite them doing nothing to indicate a willingness to change?

When we fall into a rescuer mindset, we take on battles that we can't win and have no business fighting, and we only emerge weaker and more scarred and injured than before. Similarly...

We confuse codependency with love: At first, it can feel flattering if our partner always wants to know where we are, or our friend calls us every day while we're at work, or our children can't be without us. So we exhaust ourselves by making ourselves constantly available and accessible because that's what you do for somebody you love, right?

It's unhealthy to live without boundaries: you should have a full and rich existence outside of the needs and wants of others. In healthy relationships (and in this case, I'm not talking about a very young child who depends on you to survive), it's normal and okay to step away for a while, to go off and do your own thing, and act independently without having to explain yourself. Healthy people recognize that everybody needs space and privacy, sometimes, and everybody has their own needs. Be wary of anybody who tries to bulldoze your needs in the name of 'love.' It isn't romantic or cute for your partner to 'forbid' you to go out with friends because they 'love' you too much to be away from you.

We don't notice the precedents we're setting: Remember when I spoke about guarding your 'no'? Well, when you don't get into that habit, you set up a precedent wherein everybody believes they have a right to your time, services, and emotional labour. It's easier to simply not get into this habit than to undo it, so nip any selfish attempts to control, dominate, bully, or override you in the bud. Practice saying that you are not willing to do X or will be unavailable for Y. Your stress levels and overall energy will thank you.

We expect a fair exchange: Sometimes, when we live to serve and help others, we do so out of a self-conscious belief that, if we were ever in need, they would come to us and return the favour. But this is a dangerous assumption to make. You can't 'bank' a person's goodwill for you and store it in a vault for future use, and—though this may sound harsh—nobody owes you anything just because you go above and beyond for them.

Of course, it would be nice if that were the way the world worked, but, sadly, it isn't. Don't act according to the belief that you can win people's love and affection by endlessly martyring yourself for them, as there's sadly no guarantee you'll get this back. Simply do what you *can,* because you *truly want to do so,* and don't feel bad for doing any more than that. Act assuming you'll never be repaid, and if you are, great! Treat it as a pleasant surprise.

We don't know our worth: Isn't that what this whole book is about? When we don't like ourselves, we can believe that it's only right and fair that we burn ourselves out caring for other people who are more 'worthy' of comfort, success, and happiness. This is, of course, false. You deserve as much love and compassion as you put out in the world. You can't extort it from other people, but you *are* worthy of it.

SELF-LOVE DEFICIT DISORDER

What is self-love deficit disorder (other than a mouthful)?

Put it this way: have you ever been in (or know anybody who's been in) an unhealthy, unbalanced, or potentially even toxic relationship? This person might find themselves attempting to hold back the tide or lift the weight of the world on their shoulders: in other words, they provide all the love, all the compassion, all the compromise, respect, and care. The worst part? They receive little or nothing in return.

Alternatively, they might have fallen victim to a pattern of something called intermittent reinforcement: this occurs when one party in a relationship (be it friendly, professional, familial, or romantic) enacts a pattern of callous inattention and subtle inflictions of pain, only to occasionally bombard their victim with love, validation, affection, and/or praise. The subtle abuse holds the victim under the perpetrator's thumb, and the occasional glimmer of respect ensures they stay there, starved and desperate for the next few crumbs dropped at their feet. This might be because the perpetrator suffers from Borderline Personality Disorder, Narcissistic Personality Disorder, or even mild to advanced sociopathy or psychopathy. These behaviours (on the perpetrator's part) can, however, also be due to an oblivious, cruel, controlling, or insecure personality without a pathological basis.

Whatever the reason, no man or woman deserves to be held as an emotional prisoner in the eternal hope that somehow, someday, they'll receive a shadow of love again. Love, respect, and affection are not finite resources, to be hoarded and only doled out in a miserly way when the recipient is deemed to have 'deserved' them. They should be given freely, frequently, and without conditions—brought into the light, not shrouded in darkness. You deserve to give and receive positivity this openly, and nothing less.

The dynamics described in the previous paragraph are often called co-dependent. However, the more accurate descriptor (on the victim's part) is Self-Love Deficit Disorder or SLDD. SLDD keeps sufferers in toxic relationships and bad situations because they feel they don't deserve better. They are afraid of facing scorn, shame, and loneliness if they advocate for themselves and leave.

Have you ever been scared to leave a hostile workplace, fearing retribution from your employer and sabotaging your future career? Have you ever fallen victim to the sunk-cost fallacy of believing that you're too entrenched in a relationship (because of a shared home, combined finances, or children together, for example) to leave? Do you let your parents trample over your boundaries and feelings, because after all, they're the only parents you have, and you worry about the long-term consequences of going no-contact? If so, you may be experiencing Self-Love Deficit Disorder.

The dynamics of these relationships themselves are symptoms of SLDD. Leaving that toxic boss or abusive boyfriend will improve your quality of life, but it will not address the root cause that allowed the situations to arise in the first place, which is a fundamental lack of self-confidence and self-worth.

The antithesis of SLDD is Self-Love Abundance or SLA.

WHAT IS SELF-LOVE ABUNDANCE, AND HOW CAN YOU WORK TOWARDS IT?

Self-Love Abundance is defined by something called the SLA Pyramid. Picture a three-dimensional pyramid of five tiers or layers. The foundation tier or layer comes about when we heal and resolve our attachment issues and trauma (for example, we identify and overcome unhealthy attachment models we learned in childhood); doing so involves integrating and forgiving our inner child for experiencing pain and reacting to it, as any hurt child would.

This is a process that can be worked through and explored at much greater length with a licensed therapist, but it boils down to this: imagine that you have a 'young' self and an 'adult' self. Your young self acts and emotes based on your attachment model, sometimes lashing out with pain or insecurity; your adult self regulates its behaviour and reactions based on societal expectations and desired outcomes—even when this means stifling your emotions and truth. As you can see, tipping too far towards one or the other causes you to live an inauthentic, less-than-ideal life. The trick is to nourish your inner child and treat it with compassion—in other words, reparent yourself.

The second tier of the SLA pyramid involves working towards an empowered but realistic definition of the self. This might be achieved through affirmations like, "I am who I am, and who I am is worthy of love and respect. I don't need to change to deserve affection and compassion." An empowered but realistic definition of self builds on the work done when building the foundational layer of your SLA pyramid: having forgiven and integrated your inner child, you must now acknowledge, see, and respect yourself as a whole, and recognize that, even flawed, as we all are, you are worthy. Why should you be the only person in this world who demands perfection? The answer is, of course, that you're not—but we can trick ourselves into believing that this is the case when we suffer from SLDD.

The third tier of the SLA pyramid is achieved when we accomplish existential peace: we realize that we are comfortable in our own skin as imperfect beings. Can you see how each layer builds on the previous? The fourth tier of the SLA pyramid comes about when our self-love becomes apparent and nourishes mutually reciprocal and respectful relationships. Our self-love, self-respect, and self-care spreads outwards, positively influencing others to love themselves in the same way. Our standards for relationships become higher and more specific than before: we no longer accept people in our life who disrespect us or trample our boundaries.

Once all these pieces are in place, we have climbed the SLA pyramid and achieved self-love abundance. It takes time, energy, sacrifice, and a good, hard look at our inner workings, but at the end of the day, after all the struggles, the prize is an authentic, unconditional positive relationship with yourself. Doesn't that sound worth it? Remember that you are the only person with whom you will spend your entire life, from birth until death, so it's a relationship well worth working on.

50 WAYS TO PUT YOURSELF FIRST (AND PRACTICE SELF-LOVE AND SELF-COMPASSION)

One goal I had when writing this book was to share with you tangible and practical exercises to help you grow your self-confidence and nurture a loving relationship with yourself exactly as you are. With that in mind, here is a list of not ten, not twenty, but fifty ways you can practice self-love.

1. Live mindfully: be fully in the moment.
2. Do a guided meditation from an app or online video.
3. Practice yoga or pilates.
4. Prepare three healthy meals a day.

5. Plan and batch-cook meals in advance.
6. Experiment with cooking, baking, and new flavours.
7. Avoid habitual sugar fixes (out of boredom or tiredness), but...
8. Treat yourself to that doughnut, biscuit, or hot chocolate drink if you're feeling down!
9. Get outside every day, even for 5 minutes.
10. Open your doors and windows: aerate your home.
11. Exercise every day.
12. Go for a walk.
13. Go for a run.
14. Go for a swim.
15. Go for a self-guided workout at the gym, if you've got a membership.
16. Listen to your favourite music or podcasts while working out...
17. ... And don't forget to pamper yourself in the sauna, steam room, or hot tub, too!
18. Go to an exercise class at the gym—you'll feel good, and possibly make new friends!
19. Mix up your fitness regime with something you've never tried before, like bouldering or Zumba.
20. Do something you enjoy every day, whether it's making a delicious cup of coffee from your favourite freshly ground beans, binge-watching the hottest new show, or gaming with friends, family, and loved ones.
21. Be creative! Indulge in your creative hobbies, like writing, sewing, dancing, painting, or jewellery-making.
22. See if you can market your creativity! Sell your poetry chapbook, cushions, paintings, necklaces, or performances, even if only to friends and family. With the internet, this is easier than ever before, even if you only do so intermittently/part-time.

23. Branch out and learn an entirely new skill. Always wanted to know how to knit, cook fine cuisine, speak French, or take and edit gorgeous photos? Now is the time to learn!
24. Spend time with positive people.
25. Set and maintain healthy boundaries.
26. Say no frequently and with abandon.
27. Say yes frequently and with abandon.
28. Identify negative self-talk, and change it to become positive and affirming.
29. Pause and consider before reacting.
30. Be mindful in your responses.
31. Keep the moral high ground—not for the sake of others, but yourself.
32. Celebrate achievements big and small: if all you managed to do today was take a shower, or eat a meal, that's worthy of celebration.
33. Take baby steps towards the person you want to be, and forgive yourself for mistakes.
34. Look after your teeth, hair, and skin. Make pampering yourself part of your routine.
35. Make and keep regular appointments with doctors, dentists, and therapists. Protect your body and mind.
36. If you're religious, keep a close relationship with the community of your faith. Reach out to them, accept help from them, and serve them in return.
37. Laugh, since, and dance—have more fun, and take life a little less seriously!
38. Focus on yourself and prioritize your needs.
39. Learn to be alone, and cherish being alone. Sitting quietly with our own thoughts can be intimidating at first, but liberating when we master it as a habit.
40. Be wary of social media—it's often toxic and portrays an inaccurate and highly edited version of real life.

41. Limit the amount of time you spend worrying about a situation. Say to yourself, "I am allowed to be anxious about this for five minutes, and then I have to stop."
42. Practice good sleep hygiene! Have a set bedtime, and don't vary it by more than an hour.
43. Get up when your alarm goes off consistently—don't train your body to ignore it.
44. Light candles in your space. Make use of scented oils, fragrant sprays, and reed diffusers.
45. Advocate for yourself in your career and workspace because nobody else will. Own your achievements, and demand respect and recognition.
46. Make use of humidifiers, dehumidifiers, and air purifiers—you'd be amazed how much your mental health and quality of life improve when you can breathe clearly!
47. Reach out to family, and spend time with them, even if the activities aren't something you'd usually do: play bingo with your grandma, go to a musical with your cousin, watch football with your siblings. Expressing an interest in their hobbies will strengthen your relationships and help you learn more about them.
48. Alternatively, invite your family into your life: take your sibling to your drama class or favourite hiking spot.
49. Give back to your community through volunteering, charitable giving, and activism.
50. Give your home a reorganization and deep clean. A new environment can lead to a replenished and motivated new you.

affirmation

AFFIRMATIONS

- It is not selfish to care for myself.
- I deserve rest and relaxation.
- I am entitled to the rewards of my hard work.
- I am comfortable accepting recognition for my success.
- It is not my responsibility to 'rescue' others.
- I accept that some people will not benefit from my help.
- I accept that some people do not want or deserve my help.
- I am at peace, knowing that sometimes the best thing is to walk away.
- I will no longer confuse codependency with love.
- I do not need to stay in a relationship or environment that harms me.
- I have the ability to recognize when my needs are not being met and the strength to ask for what I need.
- My humanity is profound and valid.
- I will not be disrespected or beaten down.
- I am conscious of the precedents I set, and the patterns I put in motion.
- I act and love sincerely, from my heart, without expecting a fair exchange.
- Sometimes my efforts will not be returned, and that's okay.
- I'm not obligated to suffer or be unhappy for someone else's comfort.
- Each day, I consciously remind myself of my worth.

- I welcome my inner child.
- I integrate the hurt self of my past into the strong self of my present, knowing neither is better or worse than the other.
- I forgive myself for thoughts and actions that arose from pain and confusion.
- I hold myself accountable for my thoughts and feelings, keeping an eye on the future and my continuing development.
- I will not accept intermittent reinforcement.
- I am worthy of consistent, nourishing emotional meals—not crumbs.
- I know that love is not a finite resource.
- It is never too late to leave, to change, or to advocate for myself.
- I will remember the dangers of the sunk-cost fallacy.
- I am resolving my attachment trauma.
- I am working towards an empowered and realistic image of myself.
- I am capable of inner, existential peace.
- My self-love abundance will spread outwards, nourishing and inspiring others.
- I am enough.

EXERCISE

Write down 5-10 things that you feel sad, ashamed, embarrassed, or regretful about. Then burn those pieces of paper. As you do so, let them go, consign them to the past, and forgive yourself for your mistakes. Now write down 5-10 new goals to work towards for the future.

8
LOVE YOUR BODY

Did you know that, statistically, men are likely to report feeling complacent about or content with their appearance, and women are likely to underestimate their level of conventional attractiveness (Rand & Hall, 1983)? In other words, women tend to put themselves down, see flaws that others don't, and devalue their own attractive qualities to focus on what they perceive to be negative.

It might be tempting to attribute this tendency to a general lack of confidence; however, while this might previously have been true, recent studies have indicated the opposite: statistics showed that women reported feeling as confident and happy within themselves as men do (Ibarra & Obodaru, 2009). So, how to explain this seeming discrepancy, and what does it mean?

WHY SOME WOMEN FEEL BAD ABOUT THEIR APPEARANCE (AND WHY THEY SHOULDN'T!)

Luckily, the global perception of women as second-class or inferior citizens is starting to be challenged and dismantled. However, in the meantime, women are still bombarded by millennia of arbitrary beauty standards and social conditioning, made all the worse by the use of technology to manipulate and airbrush images and spread them globally within a matter of seconds via the internet. Women reported feeling unhappy with their individual body parts and overall image, but the most frequent complaint was surrounding their weight. Many women perceived themselves negatively, labelling themselves unattractive or undesirable, basing their judgment on their size.

It's unfortunate that a global end of fatphobia, and a move toward health and acceptance of all sizes, is still some way off. This is because the media obsessively pushes images of tiny, slender women towards the public, marketing this body type as the ideal image for women and making girls and young women everywhere feel bad about themselves when they can't obtain the same. Our current (questionable) 'girl boss' wave of feminism, which puts pressure on us to 'have it all' and be fit, beautiful, powerful career women, mothers, and lovers, also adds to the societal pressure to look or be a certain way, no matter our numerous obligations, responsibilities, or health status. No wonder it's hard to feel good about ourselves!

Media and society also tend to pit women against women. Cosmetics, clothes, hair products, and razors are marketed to us with the promise that, by using them, we can become 'more attractive' than our sisters, neighbours, colleagues, etc. Advertisers take advantage of insecurity and social pressure and manipulate them toward their ends and gains. But remember that you are not in competition with other women because there is no true objective standard of beauty, and it's, therefore, impossible to be more or less attractive than anybody else, even if you tried!

"That's all well and good," I hear you say, "But there *are* standards of beauty that are universally or culturally recognized." And you're right. So what do I mean by my revolutionary statement? Simply this: while it's true that symmetrical or youthful-looking faces are commonly seen as indicators of beauty, and society values thin and slender bodies over fat or muscular ones, these are *arbitrary* standards created in a bubbling cauldron of culture, patriarchy, misogyny, and fatphobia. What is deemed as 'beautiful' differs from country to country, century to century, and person to person. Definitions are as wont to change as they are to stay consistent, which is why in the next section, we'll look at changing historical and cultural perceptions of beauty and why our standards are not as fixed as you might previously have believed.

HISTORICAL AND CULTURAL PERCEPTIONS OF BEAUTY (AND THEIR INFLUENCE)

Did you know that in sixteenth-century England, it was socially desirable for women to be as pale as possible, causing them to cover their faces in white, lead-based paint, which had numerous deleterious side effects on their health and skin (Beccia, 2020)? This was because to be pale demonstrated that you were a member of the aristocracy, with no need to labour outside in the sun. A peasant farmer ploughing fields, tending to animals, and growing crops all day would naturally develop more of a tan, so to be pale was an attempt to demonstrate your high social status (or pretend you were wealthier or more powerful than you really were!). Around the same period, it was also fashionable to have a very large, high, domed forehead—to the extent that women would shave or pluck their hairlines to push them further back! Later, in the eighteenth and nineteenth centuries, women would alter their silhouettes and body shapes with corsets and bustles, and the desired shape could change in as small a timeframe as a decade.

The appearance of a woman's breasts, waist, and backside would all be changed by whatever clothing and desired effect was in vogue at the time. While there is a misconception that corsets were always painful and restrictive to wear (often, they were supportive garments, worn in the same way as a bra today, and they varied immensely—think of the difference between lace bras, sports bras, and push-up bras, for example, all of which serve different purposes and produce different looks), there are of course reported cases of women's ribs and organs being rearranged, women fainting due to difficulty breathing, bruising to the skin caused by tight lacing, and problems with posture and mobility (Endter, 2020). Women put themselves through this discomfort or inconvenience to make use of what small power their bodies and appearance could bring them if they were deemed socially acceptable and desirable. The point I'm making is that beauty standards have been shifting, demanding, and always evolving since almost the beginning of recorded time, and it's women that have borne the brunt of this.

For example, have you heard of the ancient Chinese custom of foot binding? This practice is thought to have developed during the Song dynasty, and the earliest written references to it date back to about the year 1100 (Szczepanski, 2019). Small, dainty feet were considered beautiful and associated with the venerated and revered lotus flower of famous poems and media, while unbound feet were considered crude. Therefore, girls and women would begin the practice of binding and painfully contorting/ manipulating their feet from a young age to fit with this desired beauty standard.

Similarly, in areas of some African countries, it is the current beauty standard for women to be fat or curvy, as this is seen as an indicator of fertility, and enough wealth to eat well. Some young girls go as far as to use syringes to inject their backsides with chicken stock in order to give themselves a more rounded appearance.

Every body type, shape, skin colour, and mode of dress—from modest to revealing—is or has been desirable and socially accepted as the standard of beauty at some point or another, somewhere in the world. Some of these standards have been more harmful than others, and our liberation begins when we focus on how *we* want to look, not how we are told to look, but my point is that *there is no one right way to be beautiful.* There is no correct body shape. No correct skin colour. There is no correct silhouette or amount of jewellery or make-up, bared skin, or bodily modifications like piercings and tattoos.

Your body serves you beautifully. It keeps you breathing, thinking, feeling, and moving. It allows you to feel physical pleasures, like the taste of a good meal, the pleasing texture of an animal's soft fur, and intimate connections with your partner. Your eyes see sunrises and sparkling stars. Your ears hear music in a countless array of genres and a multitude of lyrical spoken languages. Your legs allow you to run, jump and dance. If you're a mother, your body has *created life*, and not only that, it's enabled you to keep going and care for your little ones. And if you've gained weight or stretch marks, those are only outward signs of the miracle you've achieved.

There is no right or wrong body. Only yours: uniquely beautiful and perfect just as it is.

BODY IMAGE, SELF ESTEEM, AND MENTAL HEALTH

In this section, we'll look at body image, self-esteem, and mental health. As you learned in the previous section, which dealt with cultural and historical perceptions of beauty and how they've changed over time, women have often been encouraged or even forced to adhere to contemporary (and arbitrarily dictated) notions of what is and what is not considered attractive. This is because, in a patriarchal society in which women begin on the back foot almost from birth, historically, a woman's body and appearance were one of the few social currencies she could use and employ to her advantage in order to succeed emotionally, romantically, financially, or professionally.

It's no surprise, therefore, that when we're told (either by our own inner voices or by external factors like our families, partners, or even employers) that we do not abide by these standards, we really feel the impact of the blow. After all, operating under the precedent set, what 'power' do we have, if not conventional beauty and physical fitness and strength? It can be terrifying to feel as if those have been stripped from us when historically we were already in a position of having so little.

Take, for instance, this example: has this ever happened to you? You are peacefully studying at school, working hard to further your education and one day establish yourself in the career or industry of your dreams when you are pulled aside by a teacher. You are scolded, punished, or even sent home because your skirt is "too short," or your shoulders are showing, your make-up is too heavy, your hair is not tied back, or your ears are pierced.

You are made to feel like a sinner—like you are dirty and distracting and "less-than" simply for inhabiting your own body.

What these policies don't take into mind is this: the girl with the "short skirt" may just be naturally tall, something she cannot control, and therefore the skirt looks shorter on her than it does on her contemporaries. The girl with her shoulders showing may be uncomfortably warm and need the air on her skin to be able to concentrate (plus, the shoulders are a perfectly natural and normal part of the body!). The girl wearing the heavy make-up may be using it to cover heavy acne, about which she's severely insecure, and causing her to remove it (when it wasn't doing anybody any harm in the first place!) could result in her being bullied and traumatized. The girl whose hair is down and not tied back might suffer from headaches or migraines when her hair is pulled back tightly across her skull and maybe doesn't want to damage her hairline by putting pressure on it all day. She may also have some form of sensory processing disorder or be on the autism spectrum and enjoy the security that having a blanket or curtain of hair around her face ensures. The girl with the piercings may treasure them for a cultural significance of which you're not aware.

When a dictatorial and (literal) "one-size-fits-all" approach is used to police the appearance of women and girls under the guise of "respectability" (in situations like work and school), the perpetrators of these policies are enacting and perpetuating sexist, racist, ableist, xenophobic, fatphobic, homophobic, and transphobic, harmful ideologies. Take, for example, a trans girl or woman: are you going to tell her that she cannot wear a skirt in school or the workplace because society misgenders her as a man? What about a nonbinary student who wishes to wear their hair short and wear the 'male' version of the school uniform?

Forcing people who embody and identify with the vast spectrum of femininity across all cultures and genders to conform to what *you* believe is feminine is wrong because there are myriad definitions of femininity and beauty. Some people are so exasperated by these notions that they deliberately choose not to be considered "beautiful" at all, preferring instead to be perceived as strong, independent, and intelligent—in other words, not valued mainly or only by these experiences. The thing is, people shouldn't have to reject notions of beauty to be considered of intellectual worth! They *are* beautiful, no matter how they choose to look or present, because of their innate worth and the intelligence and passion they have to offer. When we abide by one, boring, set notion of "beauty" or "femininity", we limit ourselves in sad, colourless ways.

It's no wonder, therefore, that many people struggle with body image and self-esteem issues when they don't fit the stencil of what society deems beautiful. These insidious messages seep in through our families, educators, employers, and partners, until and unless we stand up to them and reject the harm they can cause. If this is something you find difficult, you should find the affirmations at the end of this chapter to be of use in your quest for self-acceptance.

SOCIAL MEDIA AND SELF-IMAGE

Facebook, Twitter, Instagram, Snapchat, TikTok, YouTube: these monoliths loom over our culture, particularly in youthful circles, and when not guarded against, they can obliterate a person's self-esteem. Now more than ever, we are bombarded with the painstakingly stylized and curated images I've already touched upon in this chapter. People who grow up online, with no concept of having ever known anything else, find their minds warped and manipulated until they begin to conflate the thousands of images they see every day with what they should look like.

Whether it's an unscrupulous influencer falsely claiming that a certain celebrity's new line of lipsticks made her lips look plump (and not the botox injection she secretly had), or a single mum who's been roped into a dishonest MLA or pyramid scheme trying to sell dangerous and untested "tummy teas" that she claims will help her clients lose weight (they won't—but they will make you sick), or photoshopped images from a red carpet or gala event (on which the subjects and photographers have spent thousands of dollars on hair, make-up, clothes, editing, and lighting), we literally cannot escape the messaging that we could *possibly* be good enough, if *only* we bought that make-up, or consumed those laxatives, or starved ourselves, or fattened ourselves, or injected hormones, or survived off meal supplements, or had surgery, or spend thousands upon thousands to look like the girl on the cover. I'm exhausted just typing this sentence, let alone consuming that messaging day in, day out, for years on end. In our modern age, it's extremely important to protect ourselves (and our children, if we have them) from the cognitive dissonance, dissociation, depression, anxiety, disordered eating, and self-loathing that social media can cause and exacerbate.

MY JOURNEY

Allow me to get personal for a second: after all, we know each other pretty well at this point, don't we? I feel honoured and privileged to have aided you (at least, I hope I have!) even in some small way on your journey towards self-love, self-confidence, self-esteem, and self-actualization. So I'm going to share my story with you.

I have a health condition called PCOS, which stands for Polycystic Ovarian Syndrome. In short, PCOS is a hormonal imbalance that affects my menstrual cycle, fertility, mood, energy levels, and appearance—to name just a few symptoms. Because of PCOS, I have an excessive body and facial hair, which quickly grows back upon removal. I have to spend money on razors, hair removal creams, threading, plucking, and waxing—all of which damage my skin in the long run by cutting it, abrading it, or irritating it with chemicals. On top of this, my hormonal imbalance means I'm prone to acne and dark patches of skin, as well as hair that quickly becomes limp and greasy (because my skin is naturally very oily). I take hormonal birth control to treat this condition, which has its array of side effects, including a huge increase in appetite—and therefore weight gain. In the past couple of years, I've gone up three clothing sizes.

Since getting my diagnosis and beginning treatment, I have had to exchange my previously 'desirable' body for my health. I have moved further away from what is the generally accepted standard of beauty in the Western world—that is, thin, clear-skinned, and hairless. For a while, this sent me into a deep depression. I felt as if I had lost a core element of my worth. If I was no longer 'beautiful,' what right did I have to have confidence, have a loving relationship, wear nice clothes, or experience physical pleasure? I wanted to punish my body for its betrayal of me and what it had become. I stopped making an effort with my appearance because I thought, what's the point? I felt as if the damage had already been done, and there was no use trying to regain what had been lost.

I was forced to confront a lot of internalized fatphobia and misogyny which had led me to believe, even on an unconscious level, that some bodies were less worthy than others. I had to work, every day, to undo what the media, society, and my mother had taught me. Now, having come out the other end, my reward is that I see an entire spectrum of beauty, and it's far more interesting, fascinating, and varied than a single set standard from which nobody should stray. I have had to deliberately train myself to love this new body, and I won't claim that a second of it has been easy. This book wouldn't exist if we had the privilege and ability, as women, to wake up one day and say, "I love myself now!"

Sadly, the world and human psychology don't work like that. We build the foundations of self-confidence, self-esteem, and self-love painstakingly, brick by heavy brick. We fall. We make mistakes. We catch ourselves unconsciously echoing damaging beliefs. We correct ourselves. We move on. We try again tomorrow.

I now regularly work out at the gym. Not to lose weight or to impress some hypothetical person with my thickness, but for my own mental health and the sense of accomplishment, I feel after smashing my own self-imposed goals and feeling myself improving. I like to feel the strength in my body when I swim, cutting through the resistance of the water as I do so, even though I'm still not fully at peace with the way I look in a bathing suit. I like to walk, not to punish myself for eating something indulgent, but to be in nature, breathe in the fresh air, and feel my fitness increasing, my body growing stronger. I've learned which haircuts and colours I like and which don't work for me. I'm learning new make-up techniques and styles. I often clear out my wardrobe to experiment with and tweak the aesthetic I want to present to the world.

I'm not completely there, but I have come so very far. My body is not, and never will be, the way it was when I was a teenager, without health problems and with different metabolism, *and that is a good and natural thing.* We are all meant to grow, change, and develop, and our bodies are only the maps of just how far we've travelled. Do you want to remain a blank page, fixed at a single, white, static spot? Or do you want to crinkle at the edges and explore the world?

Remember that wrinkles are only laughter lines, stretch marks are tiger stripes, injuries are badges of honour that show just what we've survived, and it's an immense privilege just to be conscious and alive in a body that functions, regardless of its quirks and unique abilities and disabilities.

AFFIRMATIONS

- There is no universal standard of beauty.
- I am beloved and beautiful.
- My body is the chartered map of my lived experience.
- I honour my body and all it gives me.
- I am grateful for my sense of taste.
- I am grateful for my sense of touch.
- I am grateful for my sense of hearing.
- I am grateful for my sense of sight.
- I am grateful for my sense of smell.
- My body allows me to feel sensory pleasure.
- My body allows me to perform impressive physical feats.
- My body keeps me alert and alive.
- My body is someone, somewhere's ideal body.
- There are people who will find me desirable and beautiful.

- There are already people who find me desirable and beautiful.
- What I see in the mirror does not necessarily correlate to what others see when they look at me.
- The airbrushed and highly edited photos I see in the media are not an accurate representation of femininity or the majority of women's bodies.
- I can eat what I want when I want.
- Having a healthy appetite is normal and good.
- There is nothing wrong with being tall, short, fat, thin, curvy, straight, pale, dark, or anything in between. All of these bodies are beautiful.
- I do not need to starve myself to be considered attractive.
- I do not need to eat more than I'm comfortable eating to be considered attractive.
- I can hide or show as much of my body as I choose to.
- My worth is not dictated by the media, the patriarchy, the male gaze, or society.
- Starting today, I will stop focusing on what I believe are my 'flaws;' instead, I will choose to celebrate and highlight the things that I find beautiful about myself.
- My clothes are an expression of my personality and my true self: I will not alter my style to fit in with a socially prescribed notion of 'beauty.'
- I recognize that there is more to my worth than my physical appearance: there are so many other interesting and valuable things about me that make me special.

EXERCISE

Every day, stand in front of the mirror (ideally naked, but clothed is fine if naked makes you too uncomfortable) and thank your body for everything it's given you and everything it does. Use the affirmations in this chapter if you get stuck.

FINAL WORDS

As we come to the close of this volume, I'd like to leave you with a series of powerful self-guided meditations, to be read out loud or in your head, that you can turn to whenever you're consumed with doubts, or concerns about your progress, or simply having a bad day. We'll revisit some of the most pertinent points from the previous chapters, and I've done my very best to leave you with some fresh wisdom, insight, and inspiration.

It's been an honour to serve as a small part in your journey toward self-love. I wish you all the very best for the future, but more than luck, I wish you perseverance and the insight to realize just how precious and truly valuable you are. I believe in you.

You've got this.

9
MEDITATION SCRIPTS TO KEEP FOR LIFE

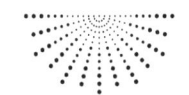

Your worth is innate and cannot be taken away from you, no matter what your circumstances are.

And it is your right from birth to be happy, feel content, feel love, and be passionately in love, with not only yourself but others.

To experience the beauty of love every single day of your existence, you must allow the love for yourself to be expressed.

Let these words illuminate your soul by reaffirming the value and love inherent in you.

Whether you are in quiet or chaos, bring your body and mind into relaxation.

Notice your attention drifting to the sounds around you... Maybe you can hear the sound of your breath, of your heartbeat... or the nature nearby... or cars passing by... or perhaps human voices... focus on only one sound at a time.

Now let go of any noise you are concentrating on, and allow all the sounds surrounding you to come in equally, so that when you hear them, they almost feel like tiny waves of relaxation soothing your mind.

Centre all your awareness on the position of your body.

Enjoy the feeling of lightness as you slowly relax.

Enjoy the feeling of weightlessness as you breathe in and out rhythmically.

Let your worries about the world around you sink away.

Feel the warmth of your body.

Feel the positive energy flowing through every space and cell of your entire body.

. . .

The whole of your energy is you.

Feel this energy within you pulsating and then settling into a beautiful state of comfort.

You are protected.

Let go of any negative thoughts regarding past decisions, past experiences and agonies.

At this moment, accept yourself just as you are.

At this moment, you are real with yourself and with others.

Your current self-awareness fosters openness.

Take slow deep breaths.

The deeper you breathe, the more you experience peace and calmness to your core.

Feel your body. Love your body. Respect your body. Respect your whole being.

You deserve to be loved, so breathe in, trusting the feelings of inner worthiness.

Set aside the judgements of others,

breathe out and accept yourself wholeheartedly.

You have always been special and valuable.

Replace old thoughts with new possibilities.

Replace old fears with new choices-

choices about how you want to live your life right now.

In your power, you are at peace.

You are open to new creations.

You are ready to create. In a sense, you are at one with the universe.

You're lying in your quality.

You are immersed in new opportunities, resting in your greater consciousness.

☀ IT'S TIME TO TAKE MY DESTINY INTO MY OWN HANDS...

Today is the first day of the rest of my life. In the past, I, like many others, have encountered hardships, trials, and tribulations.

It's natural and expected that they've affected my self-esteem, self-confidence, and self-love. But what has been lost can be regained.

I am not responsible for how I have reacted to challenges in days and years behind me because yesterday is already long gone. I am, however, responsible and accountable for how I move forward in the world. I am capable of overcoming trauma, abuse, obstacles, and the difficult relationship with myself these things have caused.

I deserve a rich and healthy future, one in which I've confronted my demons, achieved an abundance of self-love, and no longer dance to anybody's tune but my own. I deserve familial, romantic, creative, spiritual, and professional fulfilment, and the path towards all these things begins today with me.

I understand that the journey will be difficult. I also understand that progress is not linear: I am not a failure on days when my mental health is two steps forward, one step back. That is just how growth works. A very young child has to learn to crawl before she can walk, walk before she can run, and she will fall in the process—as I will fall sometimes in my journey towards my ideal self. That's more than okay—it's what's supposed to happen.

I am enough. I'm ready.

☀ I UNDERSTAND THE IMPORTANCE OF SELF-CONFIDENCE, SELF-LOVE, AND SELF-ESTEEM

Before, I might have thought it was possible to exist without these things, but I realize now that they are essential, and my relationship with myself is the only one I will be in for the entirety of my life—and because of this, it's worth working on.

I will return to this book, reabsorbing and harnessing the power of positive affirmations and mantras, revisiting the most powerful and pertinent chapters. Throughout my journey, I will frequently commit pen to paper, completing the practical exercises in each chapter, and perhaps even doing my own freeform journaling, poetry, and creative writing—whatever therapeutic endeavour is the most effective remedy, and whichever suits me best.

I realize that, while I am a flawed human being, I am still worthy of self-confidence, esteem, and an abundance of self-love. When I have worked on and achieved these for myself, they will, in turn, engender respect, admiration, and love in others.

The beauty is that by the time these blessings arrive, I will be strong enough in myself to cherish them but not need them in order to feel whole. I will understand that I am already whole, functioning, and perfectly imperfect myself, regardless of what other people may think of me or how I may externally be received.

I am excited to dig into my thought processes, feelings, reactions, and attitudes. I invite growth.

☀ I AM PREPARED TO SEE MYSELF FOR WHO I TRULY AM

I recognize that this may involve confronting some difficult or even traumatic memories from the past in order to analyze why they've affected the way I continue to think and feel in the present.

I know that I am safe from those events and people now and that I have the power to rewrite the narrative of my life, now that I am far beyond their influence and their capacity to hurt me.

I must ready myself for the fact that deep and meaningful self-interrogation may reveal things that I don't like or that I'm not proud of. I may have lashed out at others in fear, pain, and anger. I may have projected my insecurities onto other people—particularly women. I may have indulged in envy and spite instead of realizing that the positive traits and material things other people possess do not detract from my own emotional and practical wealth.

I must walk the line between forgiving myself and remaining accountable for my actions, words, thoughts, feelings, and reactions in the future. I will consciously proceed with kindness and compassion every day, extending to myself the same grace that I extend to others.

I know now that the only way to become my ideal self is to closely examine the things that have been holding me back and decisively extract them from my life, whether those things are memories, traits of my own, or toxic, manipulative people.

☀ I BELIEVE IN MY CAPABILITIES

I already have inside of me what it takes to be a good daughter, mother, grandmother, sister, aunt, niece, or cousin. I already possess the qualities that make me a good romantic partner. I am already physically attractive and beautiful in my own unique way. I have the intelligence, acumen, and determination to succeed in my chosen profession if I have one. I am a creative soul with passions, hobbies, artistic talent, and drive.

Perhaps the difficult part for me, instead of identifying these positive traits, will be to recognize and own them without shame or apology and to learn to accept praise and love for them from others around me.

The mistakes of the past do not define my future, and I am capable of anything I set my mind to. I know that there will be numerous sacrifices along the way, but I trust in my instinct and judgment to guide me faithfully through the murky waters of life.

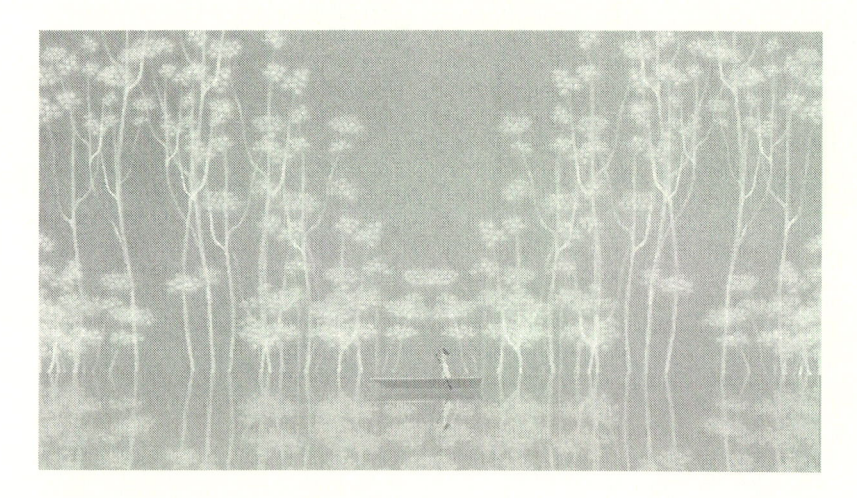

There are people in my life who will love and support me on my road towards self-actualization, offering equal parts encouragement and constructive criticism when they are needed. I will thank them for their truth and take their honest feedback on board, knowing that they have my best intentions at heart.

At the same time, I will not allow myself to be beaten down by negative people: those who would see me failing or unhappy for their satisfaction. I have the wisdom to tell the difference.

☀ I HAVE A VOICE, AND I AM GOING TO USE IT LOUDLY, PROUDLY, AND WITHOUT APOLOGY

I'LL NOT BE SILENT

When I see injustice in the world—whether it's racism, sexism, classism, homophobia, transphobia, fatphobia, xenophobia, or any other kind of hateful bigotry—I will use my newfound confidence and self-esteem to speak, not only for me but for others without the courage, privilege, or ability to speak up for themselves. I stand firmly, not just for equality but also for equity, which addresses structural imbalances in the world.

I know that my words hold the power to change the world on both an intimate and global scale and that each of these accomplishments is as valid as the other.

If today, I use my voice to speak up only to myself—correcting myself on a harmful thought or addressing my own biases and privileges—then I have done good work.

If today, I use my voice to speak out about a huge international injustice, I have also done good work.

These are not mutually exclusive concepts or actions, and they can exist side by side as I work on healing both myself and the world around me. I cannot do it all by myself, but I can use my voice to enlist the support of others who care both about me and causes passionate to my heart.

My thoughts shape my reality, and I have the power to rewrite my thoughts before I speak them out loud.

☀ THERE ARE THINGS IN THIS
WORLD THAT FRIGHTEN ME...

NO FEAR

And that's okay.

It is natural and endearingly, achingly human to be afraid, sometimes. I understand now that fear once served a very important evolutionary purpose. Fear kept my ancestors alive when they heard the rustling of predators in the bushes. Fear heightened their sense of hearing and helped them to escape.

Fear gives me the edge and rush of adrenaline that I need to succeed in my big presentation. Fear makes me an attentive, alert carer and gives me the ability to protect my young from things that may cause them harm. Fear works hand in hand with the survival instinct that has kept women alive for millennia in a world that's hostile towards us.

But fear is also nothing more than a tool. I have the power and autonomy to rise to it, use it, ignore it, or overcome it. I know now that sometimes fear means I'm on the right path. Fear only means that the stakes matter, and what kind of life would I be living if I didn't have people and goals I cared about enough to fear losing them?

Fear is an indicator that I am still breathing, still living, still fighting. It is not the enemy.

Fear, like pain, is just a message from my body and mind about my current surroundings and situation. I can heed the message. More importantly, I can take charge of my response.

☀ SELF-COMPASSION CAN BE DIFFICULT

It takes an active effort, every day, to work on my realistic, compassionate perception of self. I have to incorporate my flaws into my self-image without vilifying myself for them and without holding myself to unattainable, unfair standards of perfection.

Nobody else in this world is required to be perfect, so why should the demand for perfection apply to me? The truth is that it doesn't, but this is a trap I've fallen into in the past.

From this day and moment on, I will let go of perfectionistic notions because perfectionism is the *opposite* of compassion.

Instead, I will embrace my unique quirks, interests, personality traits, habits, and goals. I will behold myself with love, amusement, and wonder. I will marvel at my ability to complete tasks small and big. I will fall in love with the veins on the back of my hands as I make my morning coffee. I will allow my heart to lift as I sing off-key to myself in the shower. I will be grateful for myself when I cook myself a warm, nourishing meal. I will close my computer and go to bed when I am tired instead of staying up to answer yet another email for a boss and company that don't appreciate me and would replace me in an instant if I were gone. I will forgive myself for errors in the past. I will learn from my mistakes and keep my eyes fixed on the future.

☀ I LOVE MY BODY EXACTLY AS IT IS

I realize the potent influence that the media, the patriarchy, society, social media, and culture can have on my self-esteem, and I consciously choose to reject messages that tell me I am not enough.

I deserve to invest in my body's health by eating a balanced diet, maintaining good sleep hygiene, getting plenty of rest, making regular visits to the doctor and dentist, and drinking plenty of water. These are all acts of self-care and self-love, and they protect one of the most valuable assets I have: my physical health. When my physical health is good, I understand that this, in turn, will positively affect my mental health, too, as the two are intimately interlinked.

Therefore, it is my obligation to myself and to others around me to respect and honour the body I was given. I will not punish it for perceived faults. Instead, I will celebrate its one-of-a-kind beauty, strength, and capabilities. Every day, I will mindfully express gratitude for my body and its power.

☀ I AM ENOUGH; I AM GOOD ENOUGH

I am enough.

I am good enough.

I have the ability to do anything I want to in this world, and if I can't do it myself, I know how to get help from others.

Doing something about my limiting beliefs is a huge step toward success, and believing in myself is what will power me to hit my goals. My words are powerful—when I speak kindness into the universe it changes everything—and when I speak kindness into my life, everything around me gets better too.

I believe in myself. I have it all—love, prosperity, and success. I am enough. I am good enough. I can do anything.

Finally,

I know that progress is not a straight line.

On some days, I will do exceptionally well, smashing my goals, advocating for myself, relishing my own company, and nourishing the happy, healthy relationships that are important to me.

On other days, I will lose my footing and trip. I may harbour a damaging belief about myself or somebody else around me. I may feel insecure, and because of this, attempt to compete with or belittle other women who I perceive to be 'in competition' with me.

I will catch myself in these less-than-ideal behaviours and redirect my thoughts, feelings, words, and actions toward a greater good. I will apologize when I make mistakes, make amends to anybody I've hurt, and forgive myself.

Then I will move on and rebuild.

I realize now that an abundance of self-love isn't about carving a chiselled statue from a block of stone, chipping away into small, powdery fragments. Self-love is a continuous act of building, moulding, and adding new layers to form a better shape, like creating artwork out of clay. My sense of self is fluid and always evolving. This is a good thing because it means my development is never "finished." I am not formed of a finite block of stone, from which pieces are broken off and lost forever. I am pottery on a wheel, not yet set and glazed, and in a state of continuous improvement and learning. This book is just one small step to the best possible version of me.

I am capable.

I am enough.

I am ready.

I am strong.

I am a woman.

WE NEED YOUR HELP!

We would like to deeply thank you for having this book.

It is our big hope, dear reader that this book, See Yourself In A New Light, will reach and touch thousands of souls, changing their life for good. And we are humbly asking for your kind help to make this happen by giving this book a review on Amazon, the main place where people around the world can find it. Every review this book receives helps it climb the rankings, consequently reaching more new readers within its entire existence.

We passionately read all the reviews and consider them as we update our books. We also use them to get ideas for future projects. That is how important your review will be, our dear reader.

We would be incredibly grateful if you could take a minute, head to your Amazon account, and share your thoughts and experience, even if it's just a sentence or two. Uploading a few photographs of you and the book and/or your favourite pages will be even more convincing!

WE NEED YOUR HELP!

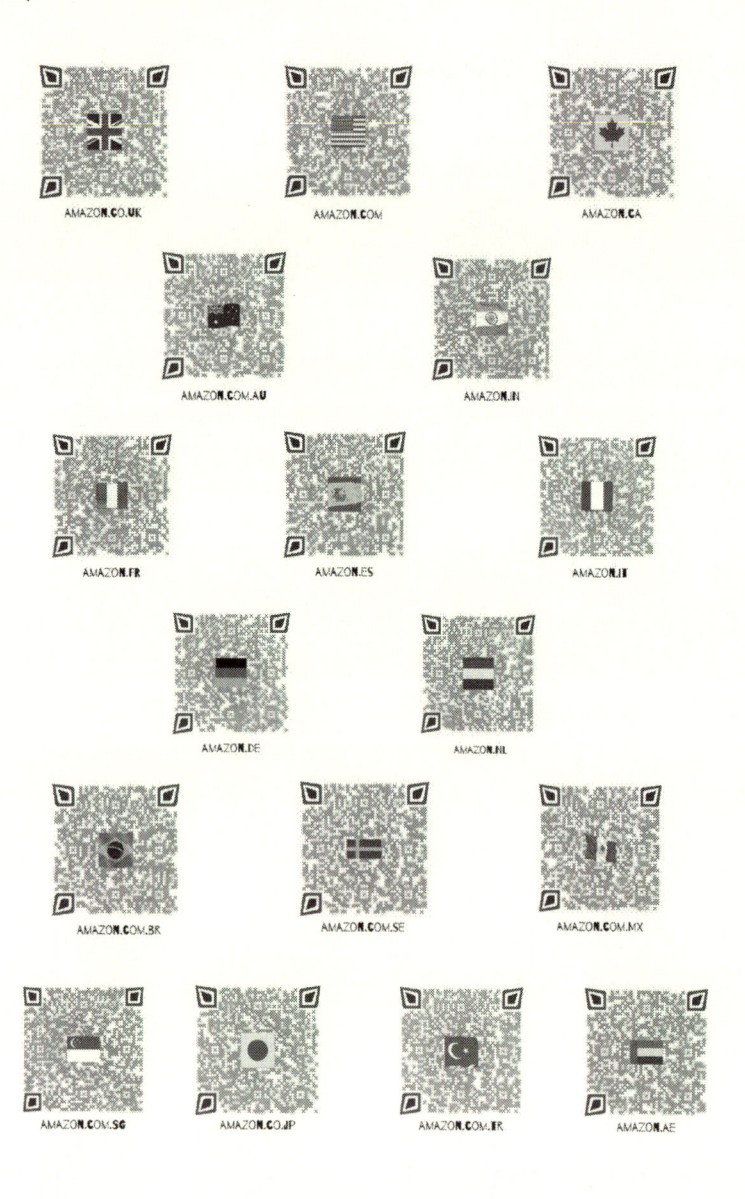

AMAZON.CO.UK

AMAZON.COM

AMAZON.CA

AMAZON.COM.AU

AMAZON.IN

AMAZON.FR

AMAZON.ES

AMAZON.IT

AMAZON.DE

AMAZON.NL

AMAZON.COM.BR

AMAZON.COM.SE

AMAZON.COM.MX

AMAZON.COM.SG

AMAZON.CO.JP

AMAZON.COM.TR

AMAZON.AE

Please select the country/region website in which your account is registered, then scan the corresponding QR code with your smartphone to get into a straightforward form where you can write your precious review.

A million thanks to you for playing such a big role in the future success of this book…

ALL THE BEST.

ACKNOWLEDGMENTS

… And a billion thanks to these amazing characters for making this beautiful book come to life:

Rebecca Davey
Rahab Fredrick
Rachel Schultz
Ajayla Johnson
Diogo Leite
Ivy Magsipoc
Chelsea Fobbs
Rochelle Gonzales
Majid Bazouyar
Faizan Ahmad
Uldson Lima

AIA

ANOTHER BOOK YOU NEED

13 STEPS TO OPTIMUM SELF-ESTEEM for Women

SARRANA RAIN

A COMPLETE GUIDE TO INCREASING SELF-WORTH AND NEVER HAVING TO DOUBT YOURSELF AGAIN

LOOK INSIDE THE BOOK BY SCANNING THE CODE

Rise above your doubts and fears with Sarrana's 13 Steps to Optimum Self-Esteem for Women. This comprehensive book will show you how to become genuinely secure and confident in your own skin by looking at your truth. Follow the steps, uncover your real worth and be able to embrace it so you can live a happy, healthy, and meaningful life without having to doubt yourself again.

Available now in paperback, eBook, hardback, and audiobook!

REFERENCES

Beccia, C. (2020, May 13). Dying to be white: The toxic history of skin color. History of Yesterday. Retrieved from https://historyofyesterday.com/dying-to-be-white-the-toxic-history-of-skin-color-ac4b5f46a52f.

Cascio, C. N., O'Donnell, M. B., Tinney, F. J., Lieberman, M. D., Taylor, S. E., Strecher, V. J., & Falk, E. B. (2016, April). Self-affirmation activates brain systems associated with self-related processing and reward and is reinforced by future orientation. *Social Cognitive and Affective Neuroscience, 11*(4), 621–629. https://doi.org/10.1093/scan/nsv136.

Dawson, S. (2021, August 8). *Learn to love yourself again in 7 days.* ASIN: B09C6KQJ6J.

Elesser, K. (2018, April 3). Power posing is back: Amy Cuddy successfully refutes criticism. *Forbes.* Retrieved from https://www.forbes.com/sites/kimelsesser/2018/04/03/power-posing-is-back-amy-cuddy-successfully-refutes-criticism/?sh=10e0aa633b8e.

Endter, K. (2020, December 4). Five myths about corsets and the truth behind corsetry. Cosplay Central. Retrieved from https://www.cosplaycentral.com/themes/historical/feature/5-myths-about-corsets.

Goodfellow-Smith, J. (2021, June 27). *Live your bucket list: Simple steps to ignite your dreams, face your fears and lead an extraordinary life, starting today.* ASIN: B097NCSFSS.

Haynes, M. C., & Lawrence, J. S. (2012). Who's to blame? Attributions of blame in unsuccessful mixed-sex work teams. *Basic and Applied Social Psychology, 34*(6), 558–564. https://doi.org/10.1080/01973533.2012.727312.

Holder, K. (2021, April). *Positive affirmations for black women to increase confidence and self-love.* ASIN: B093DWB1BG.

Ibarra, H., & Obodaru, O. (2009). Women and the vision thing. *Harvard Business Review.* Retrieved from https://hbr.org/2009/01/women-and-the-vision-thing.

Kay, K., & Shipman, C. (2014, May). The confidence gap. *The Atlantic.* Retrieved from https://www.theatlantic.com/magazine/archive/2014/05/the-confidence-gap/359815/.

Kynaston, H. (2019, April). *Self-compassion: The secret of self-compassion.* ASIN: B07QLG2Y8V.

Lentoni, A. (2020, August). *A journey to self-discovery: Proven and powerful methods for overcoming adversity, self-sabotage and low self-esteem.* ASIN: B08FBWGK15.

Lorentzen, V., Fagermo, K., Handegård, B. H., Skre, I., & Neumer, S. P. (2020, March 14). A randomized controlled trial of a six-session cognitive behavioral treatment of emotional disorders in adolescents 14–17 years old in child and adolescent mental health services (CAMHS). *BMC Psychol 8*, 25. https://doi.org/10.1186/s40359-020-0393-x.

Ludden, J. (2011, February 8). Ask for a raise? Most women hesitate. NPR: All Things Considered. Retrieved from https://www.npr.org/2011/02/14/133599768/ask-for-a-raise-most-women-hesitate.

Mattingly, L. (2020, Dec). *Meditations on self-love: Daily wisdom for healing, acceptance, and joy*. ASIN: B08NTVDJY4.

Moore, C. (2021, August 12). Positive daily affirmations: Is there science behind it? PositivePsychology.com. Retrieved from https://positivepsychology.com/daily-affirmations/.

NHS. (2019, July 16). Overview: Cognitive behavioural therapy (CBT). National Health Service UK. Retrieved from https://www.nhs.uk/mental-health/talking-therapies-medicine-treatments/talking-therapies-and-counselling/cognitive-behavioural-therapy-cbt/overview/.

Perriam, G. (2017). Analysis of survey results for My Confidence Matters Ltd. Retrieved from https://www.myconfidencematters.com/research-2017.

Rand, C. S., & Hall, J. A. (1983). Sex differences in the accuracy of self-perceived attractiveness. *Social Psychology Quarterly, 46*(4), 359–363. https://doi.org/10.2307/3033724.

Sanders, R. (2021, March 4). *Confidence & self love workbook for women: Real ways to love yourself, increase your self-worth and be confident in who you are*. ASIN: B08Y5YN52D.

Scott, E. (2020, November 18). What is the law of attraction? Very-Well Mind. Retrieved from https://www.verywellmind.com/understanding-and-using-the-law-of-attraction-3144808.

Steiger, K. (2013, June 5). When women don't take credit for their own good work. *The Atlantic*. Retrieved from https://www.theatlantic.com/sexes/archive/2013/06/when-women-dont-take-credit-for-their-own-good-work/276555/.

Szczepanski, K. (2019, November 21). The history of foot binding in China. ThoughtCo. Retrieved from https://www.thoughtco.com/the-history-of-foot-binding-in-china-195228.

Wood, J. V., Perunovic, W. Q. E., & Lee, J. W. (2009). Positive self-statements: Power for some, peril for others. *Psychological Science, 20*(7), 861–866. Retrieved from https://www.uni-muenster.de/impe ria/md/content/psyifp/aeechterhoff/wintersemester2011-12/semi narthemenfelderdersozialpsychologie/ 04_wood_etal_selfstatements_psychscience2009.pdf.

Wright, E. (2020, April 7). *Self-love and confidence workbook for strong women.* ASIN: B086WRD9V5.

Made in the USA
Columbia, SC
30 November 2022